TOLSTOY'S WORDS TO LIVE BY

TOLSTOY'S WORDS TO LIVE BY

His first digest of wisdom from the world's great thinkers

Translated and edited by
Peter Sekirin & Alan Twigg

First English translation. Originally published in Russian by Leo Tolstoy as *Mysli mudrykh liudei*

Sequel to *A Calendar of Wisdom*

RONSDALE PRESS

First English translation. Originally published in Russian by Leo Tolstoy as "Mysli mudrykh liudei" (Thoughts of Wise Men). Translated by Peter Sekirin, and edited by Alan Twigg.

RONSDALE PRESS
3350 West 21st Avenue, Vancouver, B.C., Canada V6S 1G7
www.ronsdalepress.com

Typesetting: Get to the Point, in Minion Pro 11.5 pt on 15
Paper: Ancient Forest Friendly Enviro 100 edition, 60 lb. Husky (FSC),
100% post-consumer waste, totally chlorine-free and acid-free.

Ronsdale Press wishes to thank the following for their support of its publishing program: the Canada Council for the Arts, the Government of Canada, the British Columbia Arts Council, and the Province of British Columbia through the British Columbia Book Publishing Tax Credit program.

Library and Archives Canada Cataloguing in Publication

Title: Tolstoy's words to live by : his first digest of wisdom from the world's great thinkers / translated and edited by Peter Sekirin & Alan Twigg.
Other titles: Mysli mudrykh lindei na kazhdyĭ den'. English
Names: Tolstoy, Leo, graf, 1828-1910, compiler. | Sekirin, Peter, translator, editor. | Twigg, Alan, 1952- translator, editor.
Description: "First English translation. Originally published in Russian by Leo Tolstoy as "Mysli mudrykh liudei." | "Sequel to A Calendar of Wisdom."
Identifiers: Canadiana (print) 20200188135 | Canadiana (ebook) 20200188178 | ISBN 9781553806295 (softcover) | ISBN 9781553806301 (HTML) | ISBN 9781553806318 (PDF)
Subjects: LCSH: Quotations, Russian. | LCSH: Quotations—Translations into Russian.
Classification: LCC PN6095.R8 T613 2020 | DDC 080—dc23

At Ronsdale Press we are committed to protecting the environment. To this end we are working with Canopy and printers to phase out our use of paper produced from ancient forests. This book is one step towards that goal.

Printed in Canada by Island Blue, Victoria, B.C.

"What can be more precious
than to communicate every day with
the wisest men in the world?"

—LEO TOLSTOY

ACKNOWLEDGEMENTS

The editors wish to express their sincere gratitude to publishers Ronald Hatch and Meagan Dyer of Ronsdale Press for their tireless support, Kim Yates and Colin Pierlott from the University of Toronto for their keen-eyed responses to the manuscript, James Temerty for his valuable suggestions, designer David Lester for once again being integral and Vera Sekirin for suggesting the idea to her son.

CONTENTS

Introduction

Peter Sekirin & Alan Twigg

TOLSTOY'S WORDS TO LIVE BY, this treasure trove of wisdom and spiritual advice, is derived from the original book in Tolstoy's series of compilations to inspire moral strength. It has never been published in English before. In this edited version, subject headings have been added by the editors in keeping with Tolstoy's subsequent practice in later volumes. He wrote, "I have selected thoughts and grouped them into the following major topics: God, Intellect, Law, Love, Divine Nature of Mankind, Faith, Temptations, Word, Self-Sacrifice, Eternity, Good, Kindness, Unification of People (with God), Prayer, Freedom, Perfection, Work, etc."

The text herein has been translated in accordance with the original publication of the Russian Mediator Publishing House in 1903, verified with a manuscript that was sent from Tolstoy's estate, Yasnaya Polyana, for printing in February 1903. It is this version that is contained in

Volume 40 of *Tolstoy's Collected Works* (Rus. Мысли мудрых людей на каждый день, Mysli mudrykh liudei. Собраны Л. Н. Толстым). Tolstoy's original version omitted the names of the philosophers. These, too, have been cited herein in keeping with the practice that Tolstoy adopted for his subsequent volumes.

The censors found the Russian texts of *Tolstoy's Words To Live By* and those in the later editions to be dangerous and they intervened to stop publication. Most aphorisms from ancient thinkers, of course, were seemingly harmless enough, but the censors were increasingly leery of Tolstoy's recurring emphasis on non-violence arising from his veneration of Jesus Christ. The alarmist sensitivity of the Censorship Committee was in deference to the difficulties recently faced by the Russian government to muster popular support for its campaign to wage the Russo-Japanese War, from February of 1904 to September of 1905, during which time the Russian Empire and the Empire of Japan competed for control of Manchuria and Korea.

Tolstoy had already written extensively on the importance of identifying the best path for following the doctrine of Jesus—by disregarding the rhetoric of the Church and concentrating on what he considered to be the most important portion of the Gospels: the Sermon on the Mount. "I now read it frequently," he wrote. "Nowhere does Jesus speak with greater solemnity, nowhere does he propound moral rules more definitely and practically, nor do those rules in any other form awaken more readily an echo in the human heart; nowhere else does he address a larger multitude of the common people."

Tolstoy then proceeded to explain that the most important passage in the Bible, for him, was Matthew: 5:38–39. "Ye have heard that it hath been said, An eye for an eye, and a tooth for the tooth: But I say unto ye, that ye resist not an evil person. But whosoever shall smite thee on the right cheek, turn to him the other also." As the authorities understood this, it was clearly a call not to engage in war.

This was not a message that the Russian authorities wanted to allow the charismatic and internationally-admired author to spread to the masses. The Russian fleet had recently been decimated; the conflict had lowered morale and public faith in the country's political and military leadership. An extensively revised version from Odessa Leaflet Publishing appeared in January of 1910, while Tolstoy was still alive. It is likely this was the version that Tolstoy had with him when he died.

In the month after Tolstoy died in 1910, a third version was released by Mediator Publishing. Tolstoy's death greatly enhanced the attention accorded to this work. While he was alive, Tolstoy's reputation as an outspoken critic of both the Czar and the Russian Orthodox Church made him very dangerous to the powers-that-be who feared his influence.

Newly deceased, his reputation was further enhanced by international press coverage. When the publisher of a memorial version, Ivan Gorbunov-Posadov, an ardent pacifist, decided he ought to disobey the Censorship Committee, the Russian authorities confiscated the print run and arrested Gorbunov-Posadov, who was already known as a radical who wrote anti-war poems.

After brief court proceedings, Gorbunov-Posadov went to prison for a year, and many of Tolstoy's entries for particular days had to be expunged before the book could be disseminated to the public again.

There was another version printed by Yasnaya Polyana Publishers in December of 1911 that provoked judicial intervention, but publisher V. Maksimov was found not guilty. This cleared the way for a first edition from Sablin Publishing in Moscow in 1913. Twenty years later Academia Publishers of Moscow produced another small print run. Ultimately, a definitive version was published in Russian for posterity in Tolstoy's Complete Works, Vol. 41–42 in 1932. As has been indicated, this is the version used for the English translation.

ONE OF TOLSTOY'S little-known short stories "What Men Live By" has been included to give a sense of Tolstoy's fiction at this late period of his life. It was first translated into English in 1906. It was then revised by the editors for inclusion in this edition.

Tolstoy’s Words to Live By

JANUARY

January 1 – Bliss

Brother Francis was walking with Brother Leo, from Perugia to Portiuncula, on a very cold winter's day. Francis said, "Brother Leo, it would be nice if our brothers could give examples of holy love for all the world but—write this down—this would not be the complete fulfillment of joy."

Shivering, they walked further. "Please write this down, Brother Leo," Francis added, "that if our brothers could heal the sick, cast out demons, and make the blind see, even then, this would not be complete joy."

A bit later, Francis said, "Write this, too. If we could speak all the languages of the earth and know every science, and if we could talk to the angels, and collect all the treasures of the earth and understand all the mysteries of the stars, the birds, the fish, all mankind, the trees, the stones, and the waters, even then, this would not bring perfect joy."

"Then how can we have perfect bliss?" Leo asked.

"We will know perfect bliss," Francis answered, "when we arrive, cold, tired, and happy at our destination. We will knock at the door, and the pub keeper will scold us and refuse to open the door, and we shall say to ourselves, 'God Himself told this man to say this.' When we wait until the morning in the snow, slush, and wind, cold and drenched, without any feeling of malice for this man, we shall pray for him. Only then will we know perfect bliss."

—LEO TOLSTOY

January 2 – Tranquility

People worry about matters that are out of their control, saying, "What if this happens? What if that should take place? What should I do?"

I would advise this perpetually stressed person: "Calm down—the things that should worry you are in your hands: you only have to watch your actions, thoughts, and words. Try to do what is good for you."

Do you want to sleep quietly, without fears or worries? This can be achieved only by calming the soul.

—EPICTETUS

January 3 – Eternal Life

Does life end with the death of the body? This is a basic question, and everyone will wonder about it sooner or later. The logic of our actions is determined by whether we believe in an afterlife. Every rational act is based on the belief in eternal life.

Above all else, we should understand which part of our life is eternal. Some people know this, others hesitate and suffer, and still others do not think about it at all. I am always surprised by this third kind.

—PASCAL

January 4 – Judgmentalism

Some men are prone to judgment, paying attention only to the mistakes of others. As the passions of such a one become more and more heated, he moves further from improving his own life.

—Dhammapada

Do not judge your neighbor until you are in his place.

—Talmud

"Judge not, lest ye be judged. For with what judgment you judge, you will be judged, and with the measure you use, it will be measured back to you."

—Jesus / Matthew 7:1–3

January 5 – Godliness

We either know this or we can get to know it: that the human heart and the conscience are divine, that we are united with the superior Master.

—John Ruskin

January 6 – Faithlessness

Those who have weak faith cannot inspire faith in others.

—Lao-Tze

The sin of our world is the sin of Judas. People lack faith in Christ and they sell Him for something else.

—John Ruskin

January 7 – Enlightenment

The man who laid down his life in the light of reason and serves this light, for there cannot be a more desperate situation in life, he does not know the torment of conscience, is not afraid of loneliness, and does not seek a noisy society. Such a man has a higher understanding of life, does not run from people, and does not pursue them. He is not confused by the thought of his spirit's enclosure in a carnal shell; the actions of such a man will always be the same, even in view of his imminent demise. For him, only one concern exists: to live reasonably in peaceful communication with people.

—Marcus Aurelius

January 8 – Sin

The pious men often say: the glory of our youth did not disgrace our old age. Penitent men say: the glory of our old age is redeeming our youth.

But both the pious and the penitent say: it's good for him to stay away from sin, but for he who sinned—he should repent, correct his behavior, and it will be forgiven him.

—Talmud

January 9 – Arrogance

A man standing on his tiptoe cannot stand for long. A man who thinks highly of himself cannot shine before others. He who is satisfied with himself cannot be glorified. He who boasts cannot have merit. He who is proud cannot be exalted. At the time of judgment, such people are like garbage and disgust everyone. Therefore, he who has intelligence should not rely on it.

—Lao-Tze

January 10 - Hate

Hating your neighbor is like shedding human blood.

—Talmud

He whose anger has no boundaries, he who is filled with anger—such a man will soon make himself his own worst enemy.

Just as freshly strained milk does not turn sour, an evil deed does not immediately yield fruit, but, like a fire buried in ashes, it gradually burns and torments a madman.

—Dhammapada

January 11 - Wealth

"Just then a man came up to Jesus and asked, 'Teacher, what good thing must I do to gain eternal life?' Jesus answered, 'If you want to be perfect, go, sell your possessions and give to the poor, and you will have treasure in heaven. Then come, follow me.'"

—Jesus / Matthew 19:16, 21

A rich man is insensitive and indifferent to other people's misfortunes.

—Talmud

January 12 – Morality

If you have behaved badly to your neighbor, even in something small, think of it as though it were large. If you have done something good for your neighbor, even a great act, think of it as though it were small.

—Talmud

The blessing of God will be on the person who gives to the poor.

—Talmud

January 13 – Golden Rule

How should you live? Follow the example of the best people you know. For a carpenter makes an axe handle from a piece of wood, and then compares it with that of a good axe.

Likewise, a wise man with friends will find his rule of life. He should not do to others what he does not want to be done to him.

—Chinese wisdom (Chung-Jung)

January 14 – Equanimity

Anything that is sent to us is good, and the time when it is sent to us is good as well.

—Marcus Aurelius

Oh, how happy we are when we do not hate those who hate us.

Oh, how happy we are when we are charitable among the greedy!

Oh, how happy we are when we do not say: "This is mine." Then we become like gods filled with holy light.

—DHAMMAPADA

January 15 - Restraint

Simplicity of life, language, and customs gives strength to a nation—but luxuries complicate language and tender habits hasten weakness and the destruction of the nation.

—JOHN RUSKIN

True political economy is that which teaches people not to desire ever more, but to destroy the things that will lead to their destruction.

—JOHN RUSKIN

January 16 - Dignity

A horse flees from its predator with its fast gallop, and it is unhappy, not when it cannot sing like a rooster, but when it has lost its gift: its ability to run fast.

The dog has its instincts. So, when it loses its gifts, that is, its instincts—then the dog is unhappy, and not when it cannot fly.

In the same way, a man becomes unhappy, not when he cannot overpower a bear or a lion or evil people, but when he loses his gifts of kindness and prudence. Then, such a person is truly unhappy.

It's not a pity when a man loses his money, home, estate: all this does not belong to a man. Yet, it is a pity when a man loses his true property—his dignity.

—Epictetus

January 17 – Wisdom

The whole world follows a single law, and all mankind is unified by intellect. There is only one truth, one understanding of perfection.

—Marcus Aurelius

All goods of the world are as nothing compared to the goodness of true wisdom. It is more blissful than all the pleasures of the world.

—Dhammapada

January 18 – Fearlessness

"Therefore, I tell you, have no fear for your life, what you will eat or drink; or about your body, what you will wear. Is not life more than food, and the body more than clothes?"

—Jesus / Matthew 6:25

Do not worry about tomorrow, because you do not know what will happen today. He who created this day will create the food for it. If you have bread in your basket and ask yourself, "What should I eat tomorrow?" then you belong to those who have lesser faith. He who created this day will create the food for it.

—Talmud

January 19 – Thoughtfulness

Our life is the consequence of our thoughts. It is born in the heartland of our thoughts. If a man has evil thoughts, then his punishment will follow him like a cart after the ox that draws it. Our life is the consequence of our thoughts. If one has good thoughts, then blessings will follow like a shadow.

—Lao-Tze

When a wise man adheres to the rule of wisdom, he hides it from other people and is not upset if they do not know him.

—Confucius

January 20 – Shame

False shame is a favorite weapon of the devil. It achieves more than false pride. With false pride he promotes evil, yet with false shame he stops the good.

—John Ruskin

He who is not ashamed of things that are shameful enters the path of destruction.

—Dhammapada

Shame is a good feature in a man, because a shameful man will not soon sin.

—Talmud

January 21 – Eternal Law

Evil cannot be conquered with evil, but it can be subdued by love. This is the eternal law.

—Dhammapada

January 22 – Greatness

A person who always follows the will of God, and always submits to it—this person will have great power.

—Marcus Aurelius

To love God means to move towards your Creator and be united with His superior light.

—Talmud

January 23 – Freedom

When people are worried about getting something, all their effort and fears do not bring them happiness. As soon as they achieve their desire, at once they start to desire another thing. Therefore, freedom is achieved not by fulfilling your desires, but by getting rid of them. If you want to test the truth of this, then put half of the energy that you spend on achieving some senseless desire into the effort of freeing yourself from it, and you will gain much more peace and happiness.

—Lao-Tze

Do not try to please the rich and the powerful; seek out the good and the intelligent.

—Lao-Tze

Decide for yourself which you prefer: virtue and freedom, or vice and slavery. Put yourself to the test.

—Epictetus

January 24 – Children

Be always truthful with your child, otherwise you will teach him how to be a liar.

—Talmud

Do not teach a child those things about which you are not sure. Do not tell your child a lie if you know yourself that this is a lie.

—John Ruskin

January 25 – Tolerance

When they came to the place called the Skull, they crucified him there, along with the criminals, one on his right, the other on his left. Jesus said, "Father, forgive them, for they do not know what they are doing."

—Jesus / Luke 23:33–34

The human soul is diverted from truth, moderation and virtue, not by its own will, but by force. When you understand this, you will be more tolerant.

—Marcus Aurelius

January 26 – Vices

Can you be angry at one who is sick with some disgusting illness? Is he to blame that his presence is unpleasant to you? You should treat moral illness in the same way.

"However," you would say, "humans have the intellect to understand their vices." This is true. This also means that you have an intellect; you can help your neighbor to understand his vices and bring him to a better life.

Treat his blindness, and awaken his soul, without displaying your impatience and superiority.

—Marcus Aurelius

January 27 – Intellect

Compared with the greater world, a man is a mere blade of grass, but nonetheless, a blade of grass with intellect.

A man may be dying, but he will understand that he is dying. Unlike Nature, a man may understand his own weakness. Nature understands nothing.

—Lao-Tze

Our whole advantage lies in our ability to think. This makes us superior to the natural world. Our intelligence can show us what is good and what is evil.

—Blaise Pascal

January 28 – Repentance

He who has sinned, but makes up for it with charity, enlightens the darkness of this world as the moon illumines the night.

—Dhammapada

Happy is the man who repents of his sins when he is still brave enough to do it.

—Lao-Tze

Repent before you become weak; refill your lamp while it is still alight.

—Talmud

January 29 – Truth

The truth cannot be found in conversation, but only through effort and observation. As soon as you discover one truth, two more will be instantly revealed to you.

—John Ruskin

Very often a child holds the truth in his weak little hands, while adults cannot grasp it in their strong hands, and will only gain it in the years to come.

—John Ruskin

January 30 – Wisdom

He who can see truth in a lie and the lie in a truth will be forever lost on his way to true wisdom.

—Lao-Tze

Just as the rain can easily enter a house with a leaking roof, so too will the passions seep easily into a heart not protected by meditation and thought.

—Dhammapada

January 31 - Art

Art can only be good when it serves a good purpose.

—John Ruskin

People who speak in complex and sophisticated ways are very seldom able to love others.

—Chinese wisdom (Le-Lun-Yu)
(*Tolstoy used three separate books of "Chinese wisdom" with different subtitles*)

FEBRUARY

February 1 – Wealth

Then Jesus said to his disciples: "It is hard for someone who is rich to enter the kingdom of heaven. Again, I tell you, it is easier for a camel to go through the eye of a needle than for someone who is rich to enter the kingdom of God."

—Jesus / Matthew 19:2–24

If the state is governed on the basis of reason, then we must be ashamed of poverty and misery; if the state is not governed on the basis of reason, then one should be ashamed of wealth and honors.

—Chinese wisdom (Le-Lun-Yu)

February 2 – Empowerment

If your hand is not wounded, you may touch a snake's venom and it will not harm you; likewise, evil will not harm you if you do not do evil yourself.

—Dhammapada

One who cannot read or write cannot teach others to do this. How can a person who does not know how to live his life tell others how to live.

—Marcus Aurelius

February 3 – Instinct

Even if people do not know exactly what is good, they bear it inside themselves.

—Confucius

He who has no understanding will find it; he who is not stressed about his work, will do it.

—Confucius

The most miserable of us still possesses some kind of gift, no matter how ordinary this gift may seem, and making up our character, it can, if used correctly, become a gift for all humanity.

—John Ruskin

February 4 – Disputes

The beginning of a quarrel is like a stream breaking through a dam: as soon as it breaks through, you will not hold it back.

—Talmud

Man has the power to start a dispute, but not the power to suppress it, for it flares up like a flame that cannot be quenched with water.

—Talmud

February 5 – Strength

There is no such strong and healthy body that would

never be hurt; there is no wealth that would not be lost; there is no such higher power under which they would not work. All this is perishable and fleeting, and a person who has laid down his life in all this will always be worried, afraid, upset, and suffering. He will never achieve what he wants and will fall into the very thing that he wants to avoid.

The human soul alone is safer than any impregnable fortress. Why are we doing our best to weaken this, our only stronghold? Why do we do such things that cannot give us peace of mind and do not care about what alone can give rest to our soul?

We all forget that if our conscience is clear, then no one can harm us, and that only our unreasonable desire to possess external trifles will cause quarrels and enmities.

—Epictetus

February 6 – Growth

All true thoughts are living thoughts and manifest their life to nourish and change. But they change gradually, like a tree, and not like a cloud.

—John Ruskin

Everything truly great is accomplished by slow, inconspicuous growth.

—Leo Tolstoy

February 7 – Soul

Our soul is like a sphere that is lit from the inside by its own light. This is the light of the truth that illuminates everything around itself, and in this state the soul is free and happy.

—Marcus Aurelius

Your soul is never satisfied. A man might marry a princess and surround her with fame and riches, but all in vain, since she thinks only of her elevated and noble birth. The same happens to your soul: if you surround it with all the riches on earth, it will not be satisfied because it is the daughter of heaven.

—Talmud

February 8 – Materialism

"No one can serve two masters. Either you will hate the one and love the other, or you will be devoted to the one and despise the other. You cannot serve both God and money."

—Jesus / Matthew 6:24

You cannot take care of both your soul and worldly goods at the same time. If you want worldly goods, give up your soul; if you want to protect your soul, renounce worldly goods. Otherwise, you will be constantly divided and you will not receive either one or the other.

When you are alarmed or upset with something worldly, remember that you will have to die, and then what you used to think was an important misfortune will become an insignificant nuisance in your eyes.

—Epictetus

February 9 – Greatness

Each human act is all the more honorable, better, and more magnificent the more it is done with the future in mind. This insight into the distance, this quiet patience, among all other properties, distinguishes a person from the crowd, bringing him closer to God and for every business, for every art, this measure is applicable to determine greatness.

—John Ruskin

February 10 – Approval

Heaven does not approve of our sins and the world does not approve of our virtues.

—Moritz Gottlieb Saphir

Do not consider the number but the quality of your friends; do not worry if bad people dislike you, since to be disliked by the vicious and the dissipated is a compliment for the virtuous man.

—Lucius Annaeus Seneca

February 11 – Diligence

Life is short: you must not waste a moment. Our days and our lives cannot be blessed if they are spent in idle ways. Your best morning prayer may be when you ask

God not to waste a moment of your coming day. The best grace before dinner is to know that you have deserved it by your hard work

—John Ruskin

February 12 – Optimization

You will never return the lost time; you will never correct the evil done.

—John Ruskin

The best language is carefully restrained; the best speech is carefully thought out.

—Leo Tolstoy

When you speak, your words must be better than silence.

—Arabic proverb

February 13 – Subservience

A free man is only free when everything happens as he wants. But does this mean that everything that pleases him will certainly happen to him? Not at all. For example, we are taught to write in letters and words all that we want. But to write even my name I cannot write just any letters: that way I will never write my name. I need to write exactly the letters that are needed, and in the order that is needed, and so on. We would never learn anything if we did it just as we wanted. So, in order to be a free person, you should not wish only for that which comes to mind. On the contrary, a free person must learn to desire and agree with everything that happens to him, because what happens to a person happens not in vain, but according to the spirit which governs this world.

—Epictetus

February 14 - God

The mind that can be understood is not the eternal mind. A name that can be called is not an eternal name.

—Lao-Tze

There is a being that contains everything within itself, which precedes the existence of heaven and earth: it is calm; it is incorporeal; it alone does not change. Its properties are called Reason. If you need to call him, I call him Great, Incomprehensible, Remote, and Returning.

—Lao-Tze

February 15 - Forgiveness

Then Peter came to Jesus and asked, "Lord, how many times shall I forgive my brother or sister who sins against me? Up to seven times?" Jesus answered, "I tell you, not seven times, but seventy-seven times."

—Jesus / Matthew 18:21–22

If you notice a mistake in anyone, correct him meekly and show him that he made a mistake. If your attempt is unsuccessful, blame yourself alone or, even better, do not blame anyone, but continue to be meek.

—Marcus Aurelius

February 16 – Virtue

Be truthful and do not be led by your anger. Give away your wealth to those who ask it from you, for they ask you for little. You will come close to the saints, walking along these paths.

—Dhammapada

When you scold a man and quarrel with him, you forget that people are your brothers, and you become an enemy to them, instead of being their friend. By doing this you harm yourself, because when you cease to be the kind and sociable creature that God created, and instead become a wild beast that sneaks up, tears and destroys your victim, then you have lost your most precious property. You feel the loss of a wallet with money. Why don't you feel the same loss when you have lost your honesty, kindness, and moderation?

—Epictetus

February 17 – Pacifism

All living things turn away from suffering, all living things value their life; understand yourself in every living being—do not kill and do not cause death.

—Dhammapada

Reading and writing are by no means an education if they do not help people to be kinder to all creatures.

—John Ruskin

February 18 – Responsibility

The difference between a reasonable and an unreasonable person is that an unreasonable person constantly worries about those who are not dependent on him, such as his child, father, brother, or about his affairs, about his property. To a reasonable person, if he happens to worry and grieve, then it is only for what depends directly on him: for what concerns his own thoughts, desires, and actions.

If some kind of trouble happens to us or we get into some kind of difficulty, then we all tend to blame other people for our fate, instead of realizing that if the external—independent of us—becomes a trouble or an embarrassment for us, then, in ourselves something is not right.

—Epictetus

February 19 – Universality

The life of an individual person should be completely and tightly merged with the general life of mankind, for the whole creation is imbued with harmony and unity. Both in the external nature and in the spiritual field, all phenomena of life are in close connection with each other.

Intelligent beings, called to work together for the same cause, fulfill in the common world the purpose that the members in the human body serve. They are made for working together as a team. In the consciousness that you are a member of a great spiritual fraternity, that is something encouraging and comforting.

—Marcus Aurelius

February 20 – Omnipresence

He who secretly sins, as it were, denies the omnipresent and all-seeing God.

—Talmud

He who has religion in the background, does not have it at all. God is compatible with much in the heart of man, but one thing is incompatible: that he be in the background of the heart. He who assigns God a secondary place, does not assign any.

—John Ruskin

February 21 – Work

Everything has its beginning and end. Thus is the work of man: there is not a single work that does not have a beginning and an end. He who correctly understands where the beginning and the end are stands close to truth.

—Confucius

You do not have to bring the work to its end, but you are not free to shy away from it completely. He who entrusts you with work is reliable.

—Talmud

If a person does not consider himself to have been called to fulfill his mission, he cannot be an enlightened person.

—Chinese wisdom (Le-Lun-Yu)

February 22 – Godliness

"You are the salt of the earth. But if the salt loses its saltiness, how can it be made salty again? It is no longer good for anything, except to be thrown out and then trampled underfoot."

—Jesus / Matthew 5:13

All people are more or less approaching one of two limits: one is life only for themselves, the other only for God—and thus, for their neighbor.

—Leo Tolstoy

God lives in all people, but not all people live in God. This is the reason for the suffering of people. Just as a lamp cannot burn without fire, so a person cannot live without God.

—Brahmin's wisdom (Ramakrishna)

February 23 – Women

The lord gave more wit to women than to men.

—Talmud

The good woman's path is indeed dotted with flowers but they rise behind her steps, not ahead of them.

—John Ruskin

February 24 – Suffering

Small sufferings lead us out of ourselves, while great ones bring us back. A cracked bell makes a dull sound; break it into two parts, it makes a sound again.

—Jean-Paul Richter

Only in a storm does the art of the navigator show itself and only on the battlefield is the bravery of a warrior tested. A man's courage is known only by what he does in the difficult and dangerous situations of life.

—Samuel Daniel

Our life is suffering. Without suffering, what pleasure would there be?

—Fyodor Dostoevsky

February 25 - Cultivation

All nations ultimately acknowledge the truth that has long been comprehended by those people who were their mental leaders, namely, that the first virtue of mankind is the recognition of mankind's imperfection and submission to the laws of a higher being. "All come from dust and to dust we will return" is the first truth that we have learned about ourselves; the second is to cultivate the land from which we are taken, which is our main duty. In this work—and in the relations that it establishes between us and the lower animals—the basic conditions for the development of our higher abilities and our greatest well-being are concluded. Without this work, the world and the development of his mind and art are unthinkable for man.

—John Ruskin

February 26 – Wholeheartedness

Great love is inseparable from a deep mind; the breadth of the mind is equal to the depth of the heart. Therefore, the great hearts, who are also great minds, can achieve much.

—Ivan Goncharov

Great thoughts come from the heart.

—Marquis de Vauvenargues

Our moral feelings are so intertwined with our mental powers that we cannot affect some without affecting some others. A great mind, once distorted, is forever the curse of the earth.

—John Ruskin

February 27 – Progress

An obstacle on the path of goodness leaving me overcome by the strain of spirit gives me new strength; that which threatens to be an obstacle to the attainment of goodness itself becomes goodness. The bright path opens suddenly where there was earlier no visible outcome.

—Marcus Aurelius

The law of life for the wise is unclear, but it is increasingly being clarified. The law of life for ordinary people is clear to everyone, but is also more and more obscured in the general consciousness.

—Confucius

February 28 – Forbearance

Everyone knows that a habit of exercise is strengthened by practice; if you stop, the habit itself will gradually disappear. The same thing happens to our soul's skills: when you are angry, and know that you are not doing this evil alone, you are strengthening the habit of anger. When you succumb to carnal temptations, don't think that you have done nothing, for you have strengthened the habit of lascivious deeds. A true fighter is one who fights with his thoughts.

—Epictetus

February 29 (for leap years) – Death

A man comes into the world with clenched hands and says, "The whole world is mine." He leaves it with open palms and says: "Look, I take nothing with me."

—Talmud

Just as the owner of the fig tree knows the time of its ripening, so does God know when to recall the righteous from this world.

—Talmud

MARCH

March 1 - Righteousness

Most people grieve when they lose their pleasures. The righteous man can rejoice after the reason for his joy has disappeared.

—Blaise Pascal

Give it a try: perhaps you will be able to live your life as a person who is happy with fate, as one who achieved inner peace by love and good deeds.

—Marcus Aurelius

March 2 - Abstraction

Thinking alone cannot give you true satisfaction.

Two men came into a garden, a scholar and one who lived according to God's will. The scholar at once busied himself with counting the trees and their fruit—calculating the worth of the garden. The godly man made friends with the owner of the garden, came closer to one of the trees, and enjoyed its fruit.

You should enjoy the fruit. Useless calculations—like counting the leaves on a tree—will divert you from your life without satisfying your hunger. It is not your intellect, but life in God that will give you true pleasure.

—Brahmin's wisdom (ramakrishna)

March 3 – Eternity

If you want to know the all-embracing world, you must start with yourself. Divert your thoughts from outer things and live in the spirit. That which is eternal in you does not belong to this passing life. The inner self is the part of you that has always lived, always will live, and whose last hour will never come.

—Indian wisdom

March 4 – Wisdom

The one who is truly wise is not he who can distinguish good from evil, but he who can choose the lesser of two evils.

—Al-Harizi

How a person adjusts to his fate is much more important than the fate itself.

—Wilhelm von Humboldt

March 5 – Free Will

Creating me as I am, God seemed to say: "Epictetus! I did not want to give you complete freedom to do whatever you wanted, but I instilled in you a divine particle of myself. I have given you the ability to strive for good and avoid evil; I instilled in you a free mind. If you apply your mind to everything that happens to you, then nothing in the world will serve as an obstacle or constraint on the path that I have assigned you."

—Epictetus

March 6 – Self-Sufficiency

Whoever buys bread in the market can be likened to an orphaned infant: many nurses feed him, but the child is still starving. He who consumes his own bread is like a child breastfed by his mother.

—Talmud

Your wealth, merchandise and wares, your mariners, sailors and shipwrights, your merchants and all your soldiers, and everyone else on board will sink into the heart of the sea on the day of your shipwreck . . . All who handle the oars will abandon their ships; the mariners and all the sailors will stand on the shore.

—Ezekiel 27:27, 29

March 7 – Innocence

"Truly I tell you, unless you change and become like little children, you will never enter the kingdom of heaven. Therefore, whoever takes the lowly position of this child is the greatest in the kingdom of heaven."

—Jesus / Matthew 18:3–4

How terrible the world would have been if children had not constantly been born, carrying with them innocence and the possibility of all perfection.

—Leo Tolstoy

March 8 – Meekness

When you are firmly convinced and remember that from hour to hour you have to lose your outer shell, it will be easier for you to observe justice and act in truth; it will be easier to submit to your fate. Only then will you calmly meet all sorts of rumors, gossip, and character assassinations, you will not even begin to think about them. Absorbed in only two tasks, to observe justice and to act in truth, you will act fairly in every business ahead of you and meekly bear your burden. Thus, can a person achieve inner peace, for all his desires will merge into one—to remain within God's influence.

—Marcus Aurelius

March 9 – Diligence

Be firmly assured that every day of your life is dedicated to the good of others. Do, rather than talk.

—John Ruskin

You should study the law, but also perform good deeds.

—Talmud

By not performing divine service in every voluntary act of our life, we do not do it at all.

—John Ruskin

March 10 – Commitment

The results of your affairs will be appreciated by others;

only try to keep your heart pure and fair.

—John Ruskin

The holy person takes care of the inner, not the outer; he neglects the external, but chooses the internal.

—Lao-Tze

I am convinced that only through one's personal behavior will each person of the most ordinary talents achieve the greatest amount of good.

—John Ruskin

March 11 - Service

God gave us spirit, love, and intellect to serve him, and we use them to serve our own personal goals. We use an axe to make more axes and not to build.

—Leo Tolstoy

March 12 - Truth

Not only does the truth give confidence, but one's search for it gives peace.

—Blaise Pascal

When a view of things is determined, knowledge is acquired; when knowledge is acquired, the will strives for truth; when the desire of the will is satisfied, the heart becomes good; when the heart becomes good, it will lead us to virtue.

—Confucius

March 13 - Fate

Imagine a crowd of people in chains. All of them are sentenced to death, and every day some of them are killed in front of the others. Those who remain, seeing these others dying as they wait for their own death, see their fate. This is human life.

—Blaise Pascal

People usually pay only those who amuse or deceive them, and not those who serve them. Five thousand to the talker and fifty to the farmer, this is the general rule.

—John Ruskin

March 14 - Humility

"The greatest among you will be your servant. For those who exalt themselves will be humbled, and those who humble themselves will be exalted."

—Jesus / Matthew 23:11–12

Some of your friends condemn you and some praise you; draw closer to those who reproach you and avoid those who praise you.

—Talmud

The teaching of God is likened to water: just as water, leaving great heights, accumulates in the lowlands, so is the teaching of God perceived only by humble people.

—Talmud

March 15 - Despair

No grief is as great as great fear of it.

—John Locke

There are few misfortunes as that of hopelessness; despair is more deceiving than hope.

—Marquis de Vauvenargues

March 16 - Labor

He who lives from the labors of his hands deserves more respect than he who boasts of his fear of God alone. I am ashamed of a man when he is advised to do hard work in order to imitate an ant; doubly ashamed if he did not follow this advice.

—Talmud

All labor is important, for it ennobles man. Not to teach your son a craft is the same as preparing him for robbery.

—Talmud

March 17 - Commonality

Stop talking about your personal independence. You depend on the actions of many people around you. You also depend on the acts of all past people who turned to dust thousands of years ago. Virtue does not consist in doing that for which you will receive an immediate reward or even a reward in general. There may be a reward, but there may not be, although one day, of course, the hour of retribution will come.

—John Ruskin

March 18 - Pity

Reject that which is false, doubt only that which is doubtful, wish only good, and then you will not be indignant at evil and reckless people.

If a person's eyes hurt and he has lost his sight, then you wouldn't say that he should be punished for it. So why do you want to punish such a person who is deprived of what is more precious than his eyes, devoid of the greatest good—the ability to live reasonably? Do not be angry with such people, but only feel sorry for them. Remember how often you yourself were mistaken and erred, and it is better to feel sorry for yourself because anger and cruelty nest in your soul.

—Epictetus

March 19 - Awe

Two things fill the mind with ever-increasing wonder and awe: the starry heavens above me and the moral law within me.

—Immanuel Kant

March 20 - Gifts

Weeds destroy crops, vanity torments people, only the gentle gift of humility prepares a great reward.

—Dhammapada

March 21 - Non-Violence

"You heard what is said, 'An eye for an eye, and a tooth for a tooth.' But I tell you, do not resist an evil person. If anyone slaps you on the right cheek, turn to them the other cheek."

—Jesus / Matthew 5:38–39

The person who does acts of violence is unjust; only the one who distinguishes between two paths—truth and untruth, who teaches others and leads them not by violence, but by law and justice, who is faithful to truth and reason—he only will be called truthful.

Not the sage who offers good and beautiful speeches, but the one who is patient, free from hatred and free from fear—such a one is truly wise.

—Dhammapada

March 22 - Reading

You laugh at a vain man who is having fun with idle amusements, and you think that reading a useful book is never vain. Better laugh at yourself, too, because reading for yourself alone is just as idle and vain: both of you will still suffer and complain. Why don't you read books about how better to serve people?

—Epictetus

March 23 – Responsibility

You are a day laborer; work out your day and get your daily fee. The efforts of people to penetrate into the secrets of God's existence are futile; their business is only to fulfill His law.

Do your duty, and leave the consequences with Him who has commanded it.

—Talmud

March 24 –Mutability

A wise person appears in three changing forms: when you look at him from afar, he seems important and severe, when you approach him, you see that he is gentle and affable, when you hear his words—he seems strict and tough.

—Chinese wisdom (Le-Lun-Yu)

March 25 – Repetition

Whoever sins once, and then twice, will look at sin as something already permitted.

—Talmud

A good deed is always done with effort, but then when the effort is repeated several times, it becomes a habit.

—Leo Tolstoy

March 26 – Misery

A man who would not know what his eyes could see, and who would never open them, would be very miserable. But even more miserable is the man who does not understand that he has been given reason in order to calmly endure all sorts of troubles. With the help of the mind, we can deal with all troubles.

—Epictetus

March 27 – Slavery

Diogenes used to say: "He who is truly free is always ready to die." He wrote to the Persian king: "You cannot make truly free people slaves, just as you cannot enslave fish. If you capture them, they will not become your slaves. And if they die captive with you, then what profit do you have from taking them captive?"

These are the speeches of a free man: such a person knows what true freedom is.

—Epictetus

March 28 – Love (for God)

"This is how we know that we love the children of God: by loving God and carrying out his commands. In fact, this is love for God: to keep his commands. And his commands are not burdensome."

—Jesus / John 5:2–3

Love your eternal God, so others will love Him through you.

—Talmud

Fulfill God's commandments with love. It is not the same thing to fulfill them out of fear of him.

—Talmud

March 29 – Devotion

The learned Brahmin once came to the wise king and said: "I know the holy books well and therefore I would like to teach you the truth." The king answered him: "I think that you yourself have not sufficiently understood the meaning of the sacred books. Go and try to achieve true understanding, and then I will choose you as my teacher."

The Brahmin went.

"Have I not studied scripture for so many years," he told himself, "and he still says that I do not understand them? What a stupid thing the king told me!"

Despite that, he read the holy books again carefully. But when he again came to the king, he received the same answer.

This made him think and, returning home, he locked himself in his cell and indulged in the study of scriptures again. When he began to understand their inner meaning, it became clear to him how insignificant were the riches, honors, court life and desires for earthly goods. He devoted himself to self-improvement, the exaltation of the divine principle within himself, and did not return to the king.

Several years passed, and the king came to the Brahmin and, seeing him imbued with wisdom and love, knelt down before him and said: "Now I see that you have reached a true understanding of the meaning of scripture, and now, if you are willing, I am ready to be your student."

—Brahmin's wisdom (Ramakrishna)

March 30 – Light

The sun is constantly pouring his light on the whole world, but his light is not limited to this. It pours everywhere, not being exhausted, and when it encounters an obstacle, it shows neither irritability nor anger, but it calmly illuminates everything that longs to accept it—without falling, without getting tired, covering everything turned to the light and leaving only that which itself turns away from his face. In the same way your mind should shine, spreading in all directions.

—Marcus Aurelius

March 31 - Suffering

He who becomes better after God's punishment should rejoice in the sufferings that have befallen him, because they have brought him great benefit, and he should give thanks to God for them, as well as for any other blessings.

—Talmud

What is considered a defect in an animal is a virtue in a human being. Any damage makes the animal unsuitable for the altar, but a broken heart, a broken spirit, are the most pleasant sacrifices to God.

—Talmud

APRIL

April 1 - Intellect

Remember that your intellect, if it is not enslaved by the desires of the flesh, can set you free. The life that is enlightened by understanding and free of passions is a safe haven that no evil can harm. If you do not understand this, then you are suffering from blindness.

—Marcus Aurelius

All human virtues are of divine origin. One's soul is a mirror: in its reflection you can see the image of divine intellect.

—John Ruskin

April 2 - Tenderness

Infinite tenderness is the greatest gift and possession of all truly great people.

—John Ruskin

Just as a torch or a candle fades in sunlight, so, too, does the intellect of even a wise man, and so too does the face's beauty—all of these turn pale in the light of a truly kind heart.

—Arthur Schopenhauer

April 3 - Sensuality

Music and good food will divert a traveler from his route.

Thought has no taste or smell, and you cannot see or hear it, yet the benefit you receive from it is the greatest of all.

—Lao-Tze

The most important things in this world cannot be perceived by sight, hearing, or touch.

—Leo Tolstoy

April 4 – Exposure

"This is the verdict: Light has come into the world, but people loved darkness more than light because their deeds were evil. Everyone who does evil hates the light, and will not come into the light for fear that their deeds will be exposed. But whoever lives by the truth comes into the light, so that it may be seen plainly what they have done has been done in the sight of God."

—Jesus / John 3:19–21

There is no greater misfortune than when a person begins to fear the truth.

—Leo Tolstoy

April 5 – Enlightenment

The greatest thoughts come to us effortlessly.

Great effort will not produce a great idea; it will arrive naturally and of its own accord.

—John Ruskin

Every great truth has God as its source. When it is manifested in a person, this does not mean that it comes from that person, but only that his mind is so transparent that God's will can be made manifest in this person.

—Leo Tolstoy

April 6 – Passion

There is no sin harder than passion.

There is no trouble more than dissatisfaction.

There is no crime worse than greed.

That is why a person who is free from passions is always satisfied.

—Lao-Tze

He who sets out for spiritual perfection can never be dissatisfied, because his desires are always in his power.

—Blaise Pascal

April 7 – Immunity

You are afraid that they will despise you for your meekness, but the people who matter cannot despise you for this, and you should not pay attention to the judgments of any others. The skilled carpenter will not become upset that a person who does not understand carpentry does not approve of his good work.

Do not think that evil people can hurt you. Can anyone hurt your soul? So why are you embarrassed? I laugh to myself at those who think that they can hurt me: they do not know who I am or what I believe is good and evil; they don't know that they cannot even touch what is truly mine and what I live by.

—Epictetus

April 8 – Megalomania

One of the main properties of a person is that he loves and respects himself, wishes himself good. But the trouble is, if he loves only himself, he will want to be great, but will see that he is small. He will want to be happy but will see himself miserable. He will want to be perfect but will see himself full of imperfections. He will want love and respect from people and will see that his shortcomings turn people away from him and fill them with contempt for him. Seeing the failure to fulfill his desires, such a person will fall into the most criminal case: he will begin to hate the truth that goes against him; he will want to destroy this truth, and since he cannot do this, he will try in his soul and in the eyes of others to distort the truth whenever he can. In this way he will hope to hide his shortcomings from both others and himself.

—Blaise Pascal

April 9 – Deprivation

A person has no right to evaluate complete, unconditional selflessness—much less a right to judge the results of such a life—until he has the courage to experience it himself. I think that not a single rational person would wish—and not a single honest person would dare to deny—to have the beneficial effect that those accidental deprivations of luxury goods have given him while also endangering his body and soul.

—John Ruskin

April 10 - Ignorance

Woe to the people who see, not knowing what they see, and who stand, not knowing on what they stand.

—Talmud

Woe to people who do not know the meaning of their lives. Yet the belief that this cannot be known is so widespread among people that they are even proud that they do not want to know this.

—Blaise Pascal

April 11 - Struggle

"I have come to bring fire on the earth, and how I wish it were already kindled! But I have a baptism to undergo, and what constraint I am under until it is completed! Do you think I came to bring peace on earth? No, I tell you, but instead division."

—Jesus / Luke 12:49–51

Life, for every individual and for all mankind, is a constant struggle between the flesh and the spirit. In the long run, the spirit will triumph over the flesh, but the struggle is eternal, and this is the essence of our life.

—Leo Tolstoy

April 12 - Obedience

Always remember that nothing beautiful can come from rivalry and nothing noble from pride.

Do not think that you can serve God with prayer only; you serve God by your obedience to Him.

—John Ruskin

April 13 - Intemperance

A passion in a man's heart begins as thin as a cobweb, but with time it becomes a thick rope. At first, a passion is an alien, then a friend, and at last it becomes the master of the house.

—Talmud

All intemperance is the germ of suicide; it is an invisible stream under the house, which sooner or later will wash away the foundation.

—John Blackie

April 14 - Acceptance

Follow the will of God as your own will, and God will follow your will. Give over your own desires in God's favor, and God will make it so that others will give over their own desires in your favor.

—Talmud

When you can honestly say from the bottom of your heart: "Lord, bring me where you want me to go!" only then will you be redeemed from slavery and you will become truly free.

—Epictetus

April 15 – Ideals

When the shepherd is angry with his flock, he gives them the blind ram as their leader.

—Talmud

A nation can only be beaten when its gods, that is, its moral ideals, its best aspirations, are already beaten.

—Talmud

April 16 – Discrimination

If the crowd hates someone, you must carefully examine why this is so before judging. If the crowd admires someone, you must also carefully examine this before judging.

A wise person does not ascribe meaning to words by the person who spoke them and does not neglect words only because they are uttered by an unimportant person.

—Chinese wisdom (Le-Lun-Yu)

April 17 – Selflessness

It seems unreasonable to assert the desirability of selflessness, when for the sake of so many other goals it is necessary to a greater extent than we manifest it. Selflessness is not recognized or considered good in itself, and we are unable to manifest it when it is necessary for us.

—John Ruskin

April 18 – Self-Renunciation

"Whoever finds their life will lose it, and whoever loses their life for my sake will find it."

—Jesus / Matthew 10:39

Heaven and earth are eternal. The reason that heaven and earth are eternal is that they do not exist for themselves. That is why they are eternal.

The holy man renounces himself and is saved. He is not looking for anything for himself. That is why he always gains everything he needs.

—Lao-Tze

April 19 – Justice

The privilege of fish, rats, and wolves is to live according to the law of supply and demand, but the law of human life is justice.

—John Ruskin

Only one thing in life is precious: to keep the truth. Fight for justice while fighting lies and injustice incessantly, and do not tire of being meek yourself.

—Marcus Aurelius

April 20 – Restraint

One who speaks a lot rarely puts his words into action. A wise man is always afraid that his words do not surpass his deeds. The wise do not speak empty words, fearing that their deeds are inconsistent with their words.

—Chinese wisdom (Le-Lun-Yu)

April 21 – Faculties

There are six objects in the service of man: three of them in his power and three not in his power. Eyes, ears, and nose are not in his power: for with them he sees, hears, and smells and can sense only what comes to him. But the mouth, the hand, and the leg are in his power: the mouth pronounces the words of the law or spreads blasphemy and slander; the hand gives alms or appropriates another's property or even kills itself; the foot goes to bad places or to the houses of the wise.

—Talmud

April 22 – Self-Control

I will only call a person a loyal charioteer who restrains his anger, rushing swiftly. Others, powerless, only hold on to the reins.

—Dhammapada

Our own anger or frustration does us more harm than what makes us angry.

—John Lubbock, Baron Avebury

April 23 – Work

Man's true faith is not aimed at giving him peace but at giving him the strength to work.

—John Ruskin

Work constantly: do not consider work for yourself a disaster or a burden, and do not wish for yourself praise for your work. The common good is what you should desire.

—Marcus Aurelius

April 24 – Silence

If his speech is good and gentle, then there is nothing better; if it is angry, there is nothing worse.

—Talmud

I spent all my life among the wise men and did not find anything better for a man than silence. He who doesn't pass this test errs: if a word is worth one coin, then silence is worth two. If silence befits the smart man, then all the more it befits the silly.

—Talmud

April 25 – Golden Rule

"So, in everything, do to others what you would have them do to you, for this sums up the Law of the Prophets."

—Jesus / Matthew 7:12

They asked the sage: is there such a word that could be fulfilled for its own good until the end of life?

The sage said, "There is a word, *shu*, and the meaning of this word is this: "what we do not want done to ourselves, we should not do to others."

—Chinese wisdom (Le-Lun-Yu)

April 26 - Lust

Until you have completely destroyed your lustful affection for a man or a woman, your spirit will be attached to the earthly one, like a suckling calf attached to its mother. People attracted by lust rush about like a hare caught in a trap, forever attacked by the pangs of thirst. Thus they fall into suffering for long periods.

—Dhammapada

April 27 - Communalism

Some seek happiness in power, others search for it in science, and others search for it in voluptuousness. Those people who are really close to the good understand that the good cannot be found in what only some people can own and not all. They understand that the true good of man is such that all people can possess it at once, without division and without envy; it is such that no one can lose it if he does not want to.

—Blaise Pascal

April 28 – Mortality

Look at this cloaked shadow, frail and obsessed with desires: there is no strength in it; it cannot defend itself. This body is exhausted, frail, and weak, as if it is ready to crumble into pieces; life in it is already passing into death. Is it possible to rejoice?

This fortress was made for bones: covered with meat and nourished with the juice of blood. Here old age and death, pride and arrogance dwell.

The precious chariots of kings are destroyed; old age is close to destruction. Only the doctrine of the good does not grow old, does not collapse—let the noble ones proclaim this to the noble.

—Dhammapada

April 29 – Deception

Fear ignorance, but be even more afraid of false knowledge. Turn your eyes away from the world of deception and do not trust your feelings: they lie. But in yourself, look for the eternal person.

Indeed, ignorance is like a closed and airless vessel; the soul sits in it like a bird locked up. It does not sing and cannot open its wings. But ignorance is better than a bad teaching, which is unenlightened, and not guided by spiritual wisdom.

—Buddhist wisdom (Voice of Silence)

April 30 – Philosophy

The ideal is in you, as are the obstacles to achieving it. Your position is the material with which you must reach this ideal.

A philosopher is the one who has lowered the higher to his level and who has raised the lower to the same level—that is, the one who feels himself equal, the brother of all living things.

—Thomas Carlyle

MAY

May 1 – Basics

If you love, pray and suffer, then you are a real living person.

—Indian wisdom

An intelligent man loves not because it is beneficial to him, but because he finds happiness in love itself.
An intelligent person knows that there is a supreme, infinite being on whom he depends.

—Blaise Pascal

May 2 – Revelations

All the smallest things will be revealed, everything hidden will eventually be revealed. When the detection of a hidden object is delayed, sooner or later it will appear from the gap.

—Confucius

"For there is nothing secret that would not become apparent, nor any secret that would not become known and be revealed."

—Jesus / Luke 8:17

May 3 – Revelations

Repent the day before death, and this means that day is every day. In this spirit, King Solomon gave the following parable: "A king invited his servants to a feast, but he did not indicate the time it would take place. The sensible prepared for the royal feast in advance, believing that everything was ready for the feast in the royal chamber; the foolish ones argued that such a feast would take time to prepare. Then suddenly, the royal word was heard: the feast had begun! The smart ones appeared in festival attire, but the foolish ones did not have time to dress for the feast. The king said to them, 'Let those who are prepared sit and take part in a feast, but let the unprepared ones stand and watch.'"

—Talmud

May 4 – Perspectives

You should rejoice in thinking that God has done things immeasurably more beautiful than can be captured by the human eye, but be upset at the thought that man has done more evil than his soul can comprehend or correct.

—John Ruskin

The main secret for enjoying life is to reduce the need for trivialities that disturb us and not to neglect the small pleasures that fill us with joy.

—Samuel Smiles

May 5 – Revenge

How to take revenge on your enemy? Try to do him as much good as possible.

—Epictetus

No one was ever tired of delivering blessings. But the greatest good that a person can deliver to himself is to act in accordance with the law of his mind, and this law tells you, without ever tiring you: doing good to others is the highest good for your own self.

—Marcus Aurelius

Pay for evil with good.

—Talmud

May 6 - Mindfulness

When the highest scholar hears about reason and the mind, he will try to implement it. When an ordinary scholar hears about reason, he will at times observe it, and at times, he will not observe it. When a bad scholar hears about reason, he will mock it. If the mind were not mocked: the mind would not be the mind.

—Lao-Tze

Whoever considers the immaculate as vicious and the vicious as immaculate is as one who is loyal to false opinion and enters the path of perdition. Only he who enters the good path—following the right teaching—will understand the truth.

—Dhammapada

May 7 - Evil

Evil does not exist for material nature, evil exists for every person who is given the consciousness of good, as well as freedom of choice between good and evil.

—Marcus Aurelius

Everything is from God and therefore everything is good. Evil is only good, which is made invisible by our near-sightedness.

—Blaise Pascal

If you have not yet reached the point where two truths seem to contradict each other, you have not yet begun to think.

—Leo Tolstoy

May 8 – Petitions

Each of us was taught to pray daily: "Thy kingdom come." When we hear a man swearing in the street, we are indignant and say that he calls in vain on the name of God, but we call His name in vain twenty times worse when we ask God for something that we don't care about and that we don't need at all. He does not like such petitions. If you do not need something, do not ask for it. Such a prayer is the most terrible mockery of God; the soldiers who hit Him on the head with rods could not have mocked Him as we did. If we do not wish for the coming of His kingdom, we should not pray for it. And if we do wish it, we must not only pray but also work for this coming.

—John Ruskin

May 9 – Soulfulness

"He who wants to save his soul, he will lose it; but the one who loses his soul for my sake will gain it. What is the use of man if he gains the whole world but loses his soul?

What kind of ransom will a man give for his soul?"

—Jesus / Matthew 16:25–26

When is it not the flesh of a man that is thinking, but the wisdom of the head? It will be when you understand the bliss of love for everyone, when you free yourself from sorrows and lusts, without needing them for your happiness, so that people serve you happily. When will you realize that true good is always in your power and does not depend on the beauty of nature or on other people?

—Marcus Aurelius

May 10 – Wisdom

To attain knowledge, one must examine the essence of things. Therefore, one who wishes to gain true knowledge must investigate the causes or laws which all beings obey. For those who have attained true knowledge, the essence of things and the human soul will be clear and understandable. This knowledge is called perfect and true wisdom.

—Confucius

Only that which is invisible, intangible and spiritual, and which we are aware of in ourselves, is really valid. Nevertheless, the visible and the tangible are a product of our feelings and therefore the only things that are apparent.

—Leo Tolstoy

May 11 – Fairness

The creator himself predetermined that the measure of

all human actions should not be profit but justice, and all efforts to determine the degree of an action's benefit are always fruitless. No man has ever known, does not know, and cannot know, what the final results of a certain act or a whole series of actions will be for him or for other people. But everyone can know which act is fair and which is not. We can all know in exactly the same way that the consequences of justice will ultimately be the best for others and ourselves, although we are unable to tell in advance what the results will be.

—John Ruskin

May 12 - Wisdom

A wise person can always benefit from everyone, because his gift is to extract good from all and from everything.

—John Ruskin

A wise person requires everything only from himself, but an unthinking person requires everything from others.

—Chinese wisdom (Le-Lun-Yu)

May 13 - Secularism

Secular teaching considers many things difficult that the teachings of Christ show us are easy.

According to worldly doctrine, a life that is in agreement with the teachings of Christ is very difficult, but such a life is easy for those who follow the Gospels.

According to worldly teachings, nothing is better than

having wealth and power; and for a Christian there is nothing more difficult than living with wealth and power.

—Blaise Pascal

Should we not strive for such an ideal of popular life in which to rise on the steps of the public ladder will not only captivate but also frighten the best people?

—John Ruskin

May 14 - Altruism

While trying for the happiness of others, we find our own.

—Plato

A wise person is upset by his powerlessness to do the good that he desires, but is not upset that people do not know him or falsely judge him.

—Chinese wisdom (Le-Lun-Yu)

Do good by living and dying, otherwise the day will inevitably come when you will work not for good but for evil.

—John Ruskin

May 15 - Imperfections

We love an object for its imperfections, which are divinely predetermined so that the law of human life is an effort, and the law of a human court has mercy. Only God has completeness and, the more perfect our human mind becomes, the better we feel the limitlessness in this respect and the difference between divine and human deeds.

—John Ruskin

May 16 – Mastery

"These people draw near to me with their lips, but their hearts are far from me. In vain they honor me, their teaching are merely human rules."

—Jesus / Matthew 15:8–9

To whom will we liken a man of knowledge and a loving God? To the master with an instrument of skill in his hands, a man of knowledge, whose heart is not warmed by love for God? Or a master without tools, loving God, but alien to knowledge, a man who owns an instrument, but does not know its skill.

—Talmud

May 17 – Handiwork

It is physically impossible for true religious knowledge or pure morality to exist in those classes of the people who do not earn their bread by the labor of their hands.

No one can teach anything worth knowing, other than the work of hands. The bread of life can be obtained from the shells surrounding the grain only when you grate them with your own hands.

—John Ruskin

May 18 – Strife

Do not be rude and harsh to anyone, for they can easily turn to you with the same thing; rage leads to suffering and they will respond with a blow.

—Dhammapada

Greet everyone nicely. It is not enough to keep peace only on occasion and not to engage in quarrels with one's neighbor or to answer his greeting. No, peace should be prepared, strife and discord should be prevented, making their occurrence impossible, for when it comes to the need for peaceful intervention, who can then vouch for its success?

—Talmud

May 19 – Self-Sacrifice

Remember that if you really want to become free, then you should be ready to give to God what you received from him. You must be prepared not only for death, but also for the most excruciating suffering and torture. And if you don't want to pay such a price for your freedom, then you will remain a slave for your whole life, even if you had all kinds of worldly honors, even if you became Caesar himself.

—Epictetus

May 20 – Good Deeds

Good deeds are not done by hatred or by hiring others to do them, but only by love.

—John Ruskin

When you did good for someone and this good brought

forth fruit, why are you recklessly seeking praise and rewards for your good deed?

—Marcus Aurelius

Putting one good deed next to another so tightly that there is not the slightest gap between them is what I call enjoying life.

—Marcus Aurelius

May 21 - Glory

He who pursues glory, glory flees from him; whoever avoids it, then it follows.

He who is zealous in increasing the glory of God without caring for his own will increase the glory of God simultaneously with his own.

When, not caring about the glory of God, a person cares only about his own, then the glory of God remains in its place, but such a one is diminished.

—Talmud

Truly great people have a strange consciousness of their weakness, feeling that the great is not in them, but is accomplished only through them, and that they can do and be only that which God has put into them.

—John Ruskin

May 22 - Happiness

If people do evil, they do it to themselves; they cannot

do evil to you. You were born to help them in good deeds and find your happiness in this. Know and remember that if a person is unhappy, then he himself is to blame, because God created all people for their happiness. A wise person cares only about fulfilling the will of God and reflects in the depths of his soul as follows: if you wish, Lord, that I still live, then I will live as you lead, I will dispose of the freedom that you gave me in everything that belongs to me.

But if you no longer need me, then let it be your way. If you send me death, then I will leave the world, obeying you, as a minister who understands the orders and prohibitions of his master. And while I remain on the earth, I want to be what you want me to be.

—EPICTETUS

May 23 - Service

There was also a dispute between them over which of them should be considered greater. He told them: "The kings dominate the nations, and those who exercise authority call themselves benefactors. But you are not like that. Rather the greatest among you should become as the least, and the most powerful as a servant. For who is greater: the one who sits at the table or the one who serves? Is it not the one who sits there? And yet I am in the midst of you as a servant."

—JESUS / LUKE 22:24–27

There is nothing in the world more tender and compliant than water, but meanwhile, when it attacks anything hard, nothing can be stronger than it. The weak defeats the strong. Gentleness wins over hardness. Everyone in the world knows this, but no one wants to do it.

—Lao-Tze

May 24 – Vices

Destroy one vice, and ten will disappear.

There are vices in us that are held together only by our other vices and which disappear when we destroy the main vice. Consider how the branches fall if we cut the trunk.

—Blaise Pascal

If anyone is capable of angering you, this person becomes your master; he can anger you only when you permit yourself to be angered. People are not disturbed by things but by the view they take of them. You cannot choose the external circumstances, but you can fight the evil and anger in yourself.

—Epictetus

May 25 – Aim

As a shooter directs an arrow, so a sage straightens his unstable and vacillating thoughts.

—Dhammapada

Each of us, from the emperor to the commoner, must first take care of moral self-improvement, as this is the source of the common good. For, if the beginning is not perfect, then how can the end be perfect?

—Confucius

If a man is outraged by the evil emanating from others, and it is evil that he cannot eliminate, then he is not fighting his own personal evil which is within his power to eliminate.

—Marcus Aurelius

May 26 – Judgmentalism

According to the thoughts that a person expresses, one cannot judge how he would act with us in practice. And vice versa: it's difficult for a person to judge why he is doing this, what thoughts he has in his head, and what motivates his soul. How do I recognize the inner impulses of another person, known only to himself?

It turns out that a person cannot judge a person either to condemn or justify him, nor to praise or condemn.

—Epictetus

May 27 – Shortcomings

We must thank those who show us our shortcomings. Although our shortcomings do not disappear from this instruction—we have too many of them—when our shortcomings are known to us, they begin to disturb our soul. They do not let our conscience stall and we try to correct ourselves in order to be free of them.

—Blaise Pascal

The mind of a fool can realize his own foolishness but he who is firmly convinced of his wisdom is already truly mad.

A fool will spend his whole life beside the wise and know no truth at all, as a spoon will never understand the taste of food.

—Dhammapada

May 28 – God

Whether the righteous pursues the righteous, or the villain pursues the righteous, or the villain pursues the villain, even if the righteous pursues the villain, always God intercedes for the persecuted person no matter who he is, whether he is a righteous man or a villain.

—Talmud

Only those who are equal to him and those who are higher than him can fully appreciate a person. Nevertheless, only God knows the true and unique in man.

—John Ruskin

May 29 – Miscellany

Remember that the distinguishing feature of a rational being is the free submission to its fate and not the shameful struggle with it that is inherent in animals.

—Marcus Aurelius

Who is wise? Everyone is learning something.
Who is strong? He who is himself restraining.
Who is rich? He who is satisfied with his fate.

—Talmud

Which is closer to us—our name or our body? Which is closer—our body or our wealth? What is harder to experience—gain or loss? He who has much can lose more. He who is satisfied will not tolerate humiliation. He who knows his limits will not perish.

—Lao-Tze

May 30 – Reaping

"Now listen, you rich people, weep and wail because of the misery that is coming to you. Your wealth has rotted, and moths have eaten your clothes. Your gold and silver are corroded. Their corrosion will testify against you and eat your flesh like fire. You have hoarded wealth in the last days. Look! The wages you failed to pay the workers who mowed your fields are crying out against you. The cries of the harvesters have reached the ears of the Lord Almighty."

—Jesus / James 5:1–4

May 31 – Patience

To learn patience, you need to practise almost as much as when studying music, but meanwhile we almost always scrimp when our teacher comes.

—John Ruskin

JUNE

June 1 – Constancy

Do not despair if you cannot reach all your goals or all the good things you want to achieve. If you fall, you must get up again; bear humbly your life's challenges and return to your foundation.

—Marcus Aurelius

It is easy to live as a shameless person: a boaster, a sly man, a detractor, an idler and a loafer; the life of the humble one, who constantly strives for the immaculate, is always meek, intelligent, disinterested.

—Dhammapada

Be assured that no change for the better can be accomplished quickly and easily, either by bad or good people, without considerable suffering and effort.

—John Ruskin

June 2 – Perseverance

What is unclear should be clarified. What is difficult to do should be done with great perseverance.

—Confucius

The search for truth is not a leisurely pleasure: it demands energy and effort, and you must do it. The truth is revealed to you, but you don't pay attention to it. Look for the truth. It wants you to find it.

—Blaise Pascal

June 3 – Companionship

When bandits are robbing people on a well-known highway, the wise traveler does not embark alone; he waits for an escort to guard him and then starts his trip in safety.

You should do the same with your life, if you are wise. You say: there are many misfortunes in life; where can I find safety? You look for a traveling companion, but who? A rich man? The king himself? But they can be attacked by the robbers and can be killed.

The wise man would say that the safest way is to always follow God.

Yet, what does it mean to follow God?

It means to do what He wants, and not do what He does not want.

And how to achieve this? Think and follow the law that is inscribed in your own soul.

—Epictetus

June 4 – Failings

Since the time when flattery was invented, laws have been broken and moral values have fallen.

—Talmud

It is not the seas that separate people but ignorance; not difference in languages but the feeling of animosity.

—John Ruskin

June 5 – Self-Delusion

Nature never allows a great truth to be revealed to someone who, foreseeing its consequences, refuses it. Such a person is already in the grip of a great seducer and wants to deceive himself more and more with every further effort, and believe in the justice of his error.

—John Ruskin

June 6 – Charity

"Be careful not to practice your righteousness in front of others to be seen by them. If you do, you will have no reward from your Father in heaven. So when you give to the needy, do not announce it with trumpets, as the hypocrites do in the synagogues and on the streets, to be honored by others. Truly I tell you, they have received their reward in full."

—Jesus / Matthew 6:1–2

When you are condemned for performing a good deed, this could be the highest virtue for you.

—Marcus Aurelius

June 7 – Subordination

If you do not expect anything and do not want to receive

anything from other people, they cannot fear you—in the way a bee is not afraid of another bee, and a horse is not afraid of another horse. But if your happiness lies in the power of others, you will certainly be afraid of people.

From this we must renounce everything not belonging to us, so it is not our master. We must renounce attachment to our body and to everything necessary for this: the love of wealth, fame, position and honors.

We do not need to destroy human violence with violence. Here is the prison; what harm is it to me, my soul, because it stands? Why should I destroy it? Why attack and kill people who produce violence? Their prisons, chains, and weapons will not enslave my spirit. They can take my body, but my spirit is free. No one can interfere with it, and so I live as I want.

How did I reach this point? I subordinated my will to that of God. If he wants me to have a fever, I want that. If he wants me to do this, or not that, I want that. If he wants something to happen to me, I want that. If he does not want, so I do not want. If he wants me to die or be tortured, I want to die and endure torture.

—Epictetus

June 8 – Work

If work is the main thing for you, and pay is secondary, then your master is God. But if the work for you is a secondary thing, and most important is the pay, then you are slaves to pay and its creator—the devil.

Of all the useless expenses, the most inadmissible is a waste of labor.

The beginning of every good law—and perhaps the end of it—is that each person should obtain his own bread as a result of his own good labor.

—John Ruskin

June 9 - Fulfillment

The more you accomplish wise deeds, the more fulfilled your life becomes.

—John Ruskin

Watch yourself in thoughts, in words, and protect your actions from evil. While observing the purity of these three paths, you will enter the path shown to us by the wise men.

—Dhammapada

June 10 - Humility

To know a lot and not show oneself as knowledgeable is to have reached a moral height. To know a little and show oneself as knowledgeable is a disease. Only by understanding this disease can we rid ourselves of it.

—Lao-Tze

A man of genius is ready to work more than other people. He always extracts more good from his work, and is so little aware of the divine gift contained in him that he will attribute his abilities to the properties of his work.

—John Ruskin

June 11 – Freedom

The greatest good for man is his freedom. If freedom is goodness, a free man cannot be unhappy. If you see a person is unhappy and suffering, you should know immediately that this person is not free—he is surely enslaved by someone or something.

If freedom is good, a free man cannot be a scoundrel. If you see a person humiliating others, or flattering them, know this person is also not free. He is a slave who continually seeks profitable positions.

A free man controls only what can be controlled freely. It is only possible to control freely and completely oneself. If you see a person who wants to control not himself but others, know he is not free; he is a slave to his desire to rule over people.

—Epictetus

June 12 – Lessons

If God would give us such mentors that we could know, for certain, they were sent by God himself, we would obey them freely and joyfully.

We have such mentors: they are our needs, and generally, any of life's troubles.

—Blaise Pascal

Do not get used to prosperity—it comes and goes. He who owns should learn how to lose; and he who is happy should learn how to suffer.

—Friedrich Schiller

June 13 - God

Teacher, what is the greatest commandment in the law? Jesus replied: "Love the Lord your God with all your heart, with all your soul, and with all your mind. This is the first and greatest commandment. And the second is: Love your neighbor as yourself. And all the Law and the Prophets hang on these two commandments."

—Jesus / Matthew 22:36–40

A person who has acquired knowledge of the law but is alien to the love of God is like a treasurer to whom the keys for the inner rooms were given, without the keys to the front door.

—Talmud

June 14 - God

Love God with all your soul, even when he takes it from you—even when you must sacrifice your life to glorify his holy name.

—Talmud

Fear the eternal God of our fathers and serve him out of love. Fear leads to the desire to avoid sin, and love leads to the diligent fulfillment of God's commandments.

—Talmud

June 15 – Freedom

Look at how the slave wants to live. He wants to be released into the wild. He thinks that without this, he can neither be free nor happy. He says this: if they let me go free, I would be very happy right now. I would not be forced to please and serve my master, I could talk to anyone as an equal. I could go wherever I want, without asking anyone.

As soon as they let him out, he immediately looks for someone to flatter for lunch, because the owner no longer feeds him. For this, he is ready to go to all sorts of abominations. As soon as he finds an apartment and food, he will again fall into slavery—more severe than before.

If such a person begins to grow rich, he now has a lover, usually some extravagant woman. And so, he begins to suffer and cry. When it is especially difficult for him, he recalls his former slavery and says:

But I didn't feel bad with my master! I didn't take care of myself, but they dressed me, put on shoes, fed me. When I was sick, they took care of me. The service was not difficult. I had one owner, and now, how many of them I have! How many people should I please in order to get rich?

But the slave will not come to his senses. He wants to grow rich, and for this he suffers all sorts of hardships. When he gets what he wanted, then again, it turns out that he upbraided himself with unpleasant worries.

Still, he thinks: if I became a great commander, all my misfortunes would end. They would carry me in their arms! And he goes on campaigns. He suffers all sorts of hardships, suffers as a hard laborer, yet he asks for a campaign for the second and third time. If he wants to get rid of his troubles and misfortunes, let him first come to his senses. Let him know what the true blessing of life is. May he act at every step of life according to the laws of truth and goodness inscribed in his soul, and gain true freedom.

—EPICTETUS

June 16 – Freedom

To be a person of high morality means to have a free soul. People who are constantly angry at someone, who are constantly afraid of something and completely surrendering to passions, cannot be free in their soul. They cannot concentrate on themselves and are constantly fond of something external. That person sees—and cannot see, hears—and cannot hear, tastes—and cannot distinguish taste.

—CONFUCIUS

Those who are engulfed in the flames of passionate desires and only grow their own lusts are forever attached tightly to a chain.

Those who think only of the joys of tranquility and inner peace, who depend on thoughts, and who are happy with those things that people do not find happiness in, will break the chains of death—they will forever drop them.

—DHAMMAPADA

June 17 – Verbosity

Speak only of things that are as clear as the morning to you; otherwise, keep silent.

—Talmud

The wisest teachers are those who do not argue.

—John Ruskin

A wise person may be considered truly wise for just one word uttered. For even one misspoken word, he may be considered ignorant. A truly wise person is cautious in his words.

—Chinese wisdom (Le-Lun-Yu)

June 18 – Charity

If you are not consciously kind to everyone, you will often be unconsciously cruel to many. This often happens to people who lack a vivid imagination.

—John Ruskin

The essence of charity is love—which is manifested when performing acts of charity.

—Talmud

A true Christian wishes good not only to his neighbors, but also to his enemies. He wishes good not only to his enemies, but also to the enemies of God. Notice also that his love for people often gives him not pleasure, but suffering.

—Blaise Pascal

June 19 – Ignorance

People cannot know and understand everything that is being done in the world, and therefore their judgments about many things are incorrect. Ignorance is twofold: one ignorance is pure, natural ignorance in which people are born. Another ignorance is that of the truly wise. When people learn all the sciences and everything that people knew and know, they will see that this knowledge, taken together, is so insignificant that there is no way that this knowledge will help you to really understand the world created by God, and you will be convinced that scientists are just people—that in essence, they still do not know anything. They are just like simple, unlearned people.

There are some people who have learned something, have gained some knowledge of the sciences and become arrogant. They left natural ignorance but did not manage to reach the true wisdom of those scientists who understood the imperfection and insignificance of all human knowledge. These are people who consider themselves wise but are not. They judge everything recklessly and are constantly mistaken. They know how to attract attention and are often respected, but ordinary people despise them, seeing their worthlessness. They despise other people, considering them ignorant.

—Blaise Pascal

June 20 – Brotherhood

"Whoever claims to love God yet hates a brother or sister

is a liar. For whoever does not love their brother and sister, whom they have seen, cannot love God, whom they have not seen."

—JESUS / FIRST EPISTLE OF JOHN 4:20

Show justice to your neighbor—by loving and not loving him—and you will learn to love him. But if you are unfair to him because you do not love him, then you will end up hating him.

—JOHN RUSKIN

June 21 – Harmony

Everything in the world grows, blooms and returns to its root. Returning to one's root means tranquility and harmony with nature. To be in harmony with nature means you are eternal. The destruction of the body does not pose any danger.

—LAO-TZE

An evil person who has transgressed the law thinks carelessly that his life may soon end with death. Such a person is capable of all kinds of evil deeds.

—DHAMMAPADA

June 22 – Effort

If there are people who do not educate themselves, and if they do, they do not keep pace with it—they should not despair.

If there are people who do not ask enlightened people about things they do not know, and if by asking, they do not become more enlightened—they should not despair.

If there are people who do not reflect on things, and if they do, cannot acquire a clear understanding of the beginning of things—they should not despair.

If there are people who do not distinguish between good and evil, and if they do, and they do not have a clear idea about it—they should not despair.

If there are people who do not do good, and if they do, do not give all their strength to it—they should not despair.

What others would do at once, they will do gradually. What others achieve after hundreds of attempts, they will do after thousands.

Those who truly follow this rule of constant effort, no matter how ignorant they are, will certainly become enlightened. No matter how weak they are, they will certainly become strong.

—Chinese wisdom (Chung-Jung)

June 23 – Perspective

Respond with love to animosity. Look at difficult things when they are easy. Address a great endeavor when it is still small. When the greatest enterprises first appear, they are small.

—Lao-Tze

Just as guards carefully secure a fortress, you should carefully guard yourself without losing focus. If you lose your attention in a decisive moment, you will inevitably fail to reach your goal.

—Dhammapada

June 24 - Self-Protection

Do not succumb to the mood of the one who offends you. Do not take the path that they hope will bring you down.

Beware not to become the same as those who are evil and inhuman around you.

The best way to avenge the offender is never to follow his example.

—Marcus Aurelius

June 25 - Regimen

May every dawn be the beginning of a new life for you, and every sunset be the end of it. Let each of these short lives leave a trace of some good—either love manifested for others, or a good deed—or some acquired lesson that you have learned.

—John Ruskin

If you suffer from the memory that you neglected wisdom and did not live like the wise men, do not worry about it. Be pleased by beginning to live as your conscience requires.

—Marcus Aurelius

June 26 – Duty

One of our major duties is to think about the bright intellect given to us from Heaven. It is our duty to make it shine.

—Chinese wisdom

Man has the ability to think about creation. You must think logically. You must think about why we live in this world, about your soul and about God.

Most people around you are thinking about everything else, but not this. They think about extravagant pleasures. They think about big houses, great wealth and power. They envy the rich and famous. They do not think about being a good person.

—Blaise Pascal

June 27 – Spirit

"Do not fear those who kill the body but cannot kill a soul. Fear those who can destroy both their soul and body."

—Jesus / Matthew 10:28

I consist of both spirit and body.

For the body, everything is indifferent—it is deprived of the ability to distinguish anything spiritual.

All that does not proceed from the spirit is also indifferent. Life of the spirit is independent, it does not exist in the past or future—all its importance is concentrated in the present.

—Marcus Aurelius

June 28 – Self-Assessment

The deeper a person descends into himself, and the more insignificant he seems to himself, the higher he ascends to God.

—Thomas à Kempis

People are like a mathematical fraction. The numerator is the virtues of man while the denominator is a person's assessment of themselves. To increase one's numerator—one's own merits—is difficult for all people. Anyone can reduce one's denominator—one's opinion of oneself. One can approach perfection by this decrease.

—Leo Tolstoy

June 29 – Adaptability

Reason produces beings, and virtue nourishes them. There is not one creature that does not respect reason or honor virtue.

You must be like water. When there are no obstacles, it flows. When there is a dam, it will stop. When a dam breaks, it will flow again. In a quadrangular-shaped bottle, the water is quadrangular. In a round-shaped bottle, its shape is round. It is the strongest of all elements.

—Lao-Tze

June 30 – Light

Those who seek immortal truth must control their thoughts to achieve their goal. Keep your gaze on the pure light that is free from passion.

For the flame to give a calm light, the lamp must be protected from the wind. If the flame is subjected to changing winds, it will tremble and throw deceptive shadows onto the white surface of the soul.

Compassion for others is the law of eternal harmony, the law of eternal love.

—Brahmin's wisdom (Ramakrishna)

JULY

July 1 – Ignorance

To explain is to waste time. A man who sees clearly understands everything with a small hint; a man who sees incorrectly will not understand anything, even if you present a very detailed account.

—John Ruskin

July 2 – Teaching

A good person is the teacher of a bad person; a bad person is the material with which a good person works. Anyone who does not respect his teacher and does not like the material he is working on—even if that person is very clever—is mistaken.

—Lao-Tze

If you can teach a person how to be good and don't do it, you lose your brother.

If a person is not disposed to accept your teachings, and yet you pass them on to him, you lose words.

A wise, enlightened person does not lose either his brother or his words.

—Chinese wisdom (Le-Lun-Yu)

July 3 - Light

"The eye is the lamp of the body. So, if your eye is unclouded, your whole body will be full of light. But if your eye is unhealthy, your whole body will be full of darkness. If then the light within you is darkness, how great is that darkness!"

—JESUS / MATTHEW 6:22–23

When the light goes out around you, a dark shadow from your own heart falls on your path. Beware of this terrible shadow: no light of your mind can destroy the darkness emanating from your soul, until all selfish thoughts are expelled from it.

—BRAHMIN'S WISDOM (RAMAKRISHNA)

July 4 - Altruism

People senselessly love and believe in vain, remaining unjust, and the great erroneous belief of the best people, from generation to generation, consists in helping the poor by giving alms, preaching patience, hope, and all sorts of other mitigating and comforting means, and not in the way that was solely commanded to us by God—not by justice.

The only thing a good person should do is be fair to others and teach the same. A sacrifice of one's own strength, one's own life, and one's own happiness is always a sad necessity and not the fulfillment of the eternal law of life.

—JOHN RUSKIN

July 5 – Virtue

People of the highest virtue do not consider themselves virtuous, therefore they are virtuous. People of the lowest virtue never forget about virtue, and therefore do not have it. The highest virtue does not affirm itself and appears. The lower virtue affirms itself and does not appear.

When the highest virtue is lost, good nature appears; when good nature is lost, justice appears; when justice is lost, there is decency.

The rules of decency are only the semblance of truth and the beginning of all disorder. Wit is the blossom of reason, but it is also the beginning of ignorance. Therefore, a holy man holds on to the fruit, not the flower, casts off the last and holds on to the first.

—Lao-Tze

July 6 – Determination

You must be firmly determined that all your goods belong to God, then you will be close to the divine. And you should do it simply and calmly, thinking of yourself only as a creature sent into this world to carry out his work, and in every free minute thinking about what you have to do next.

—John Ruskin

July 7 – God

When I tell you about God, do not think that I will be

telling you about any item made of gold or silver. The god I am telling you about, you feel him in your soul. You carry him in yourself, and with your unclean thoughts and abominable deeds you defile his image in your soul.

If only we would constantly remember that God is in us and a witness to everything that we think and do, then we would stop our bad actions, and God would make us inseparable from him. Let us remember God, and think and talk about him as often as possible.

—Epictetus

July 8 – Wealth

Alas! The deprivation of food is not the most cruel, and the cries of the poor and hungry are not the strongest. There are things in life that are more important than food: the rich deprive the poor not only of food, but of virtue, wisdom, and salvation.

—John Ruskin

It is difficult to be poor and not to feel unkind. On the contrary, it is very easy to be rich and not be proud of it.

—Chinese wisdom (Le-Lun-Yu)

Some wealth is heavy from the human tears shed over it, like a poorly harvested crop is heavy from untimely rains.

—John Ruskin

A stone falls on a jug: woe to a jug. A jug falls on a stone: woe to a jug. One way or another: all woe to the jug.

—Talmud

July 9 – Self-Harm

An evil person harms himself before hurting others.

—St. Augustine

A person can avoid the misfortunes sent by heaven, but there is no escape from the misfortunes that he brings upon himself.

—Eastern proverb

July 10 – Wealth

Has any woman become better by owning diamonds? How many women become low, depraved, and unhappy for desiring diamonds? And do men become better from owning chests of gold? Who can measure all the evil created in order to fill them?

—John Ruskin

"How difficult it is for those who have wealth to enter the kingdom of God! For it is easier for a camel to go through the eye of a needle than for a rich person to enter the kingdom of God."

—Jesus / Luke 18:24–25

July 11 – Self-Reliance

Although the sage is strict with himself, he does not require anything from others. He is satisfied with his position and never complains. He humbly obeys fate because he does not blame others for it.

A person seeking earthly goods and riches is in danger.

When the arrow does not hit the target, the shooter blames himself, and not the target. So does the sage.

—Confucius

July 12 – Equanimity

To truly believe in your understanding of life and wish people well, you will occasionally express your opinions in ways that will make your opponents believe you are in error. The more mistaken your interlocutor is, the more he must appreciate your understanding of life.

It is most important not to get annoyed or be unkind while showing your interlocutor truth in conversation.

—Epictetus

July 13 – Resolve

Live as if you must say goodbye to life today, as if the time left is an unexpected gift.

—Marcus Aurelius

Defeat rage with love. Answer good with evil. Overcome stinginess with generosity. Correct a liar with the truth.

—Dhammapada

Do not defile yourself with contentions that cause destruction to your body, soul and belongings. Arguments result in noble people being diminished, entire families disappearing, princes losing their property, cities being destroyed, the pious being disgraced, believers dying and nobles being covered with shame and disgrace.

—Talmud

July 14 - Praise

Do not refuse praise to a deserving person. This person loses necessary support towards the proper path and does not receive proper tribute for his work.

—John Ruskin

A lot of harm can be done with careless words of praise and condemnation.

—John Ruskin

July 15 - Madness

The thirst of a madman increases while simply attempting to survive. He behaves like a monkey, looking for fruit, jumping from one tree to another.

Those gripped by this instinctive thirst will be filled with suffering.

Those who conquer this thirst, will dissipate suffering, and it will fall away from them, like drops of rain fall from a lotus flower.

—Dhammapada

July 16 – Criticism

People are criticized for both speaking too much and speaking too little. No one will ever be constantly condemned or always praised.

—Dhammapada

Knowing the source of human judgments would stop the desire for others' approval.

—Marcus Aurelius

July 17 – Burdens

You must retain self-control when faced with anger due to an unpleasant burden. Peace of mind is achieved by controlling emotion.

—Marcus Aurelius

"Those who are burdened can come to me for reassurance. Learn from my gentle and humble heart, for my yoke is easy and my burden is light."

—Jesus / Matthew 11:28–30

July 18 – Determination

Make haste to do good deeds, even insignificant ones, and try to avoid any sins. A good deed entails virtue while vice begets more sin.

—Talmud

No life worthy of God's name is possible without the sure

determination in your heart to always do good, regardless of where it leads.

—John Ruskin

July 19 – Karma

If you treat people well in hopes of benefiting from their gratitude, you will not receive the slightest repayment for your imaginary kindness, but treat them well without any selfish considerations, and you will achieve both gratitude and benefit.

So, in everything: he who wants to save his soul, he will lose it, and he who loses his soul for God, he will gain it.

—John Ruskin

July 20 – Immortality

Real life is not fleeting, not easy, and never disappears. Each noble life leaves its threads forever woven into the cause of peace. And thus the power of mankind, with healthy roots and branches rising higher to the sky, grows more and more.

—John Ruskin

July 21 – Mankind

All the material world is at your disposal, and you—as a rational creature—can make use of it. Yes, you can use your own reason, but do not forget the spiritual connection that connects you with Reason itself.

—Marcus Aurelius

At every moment of our lives, we should try to find, not what separates us from other people, but what we have in common with them.

—John Ruskin

July 22 – Self-Control

He who destroys living beings, speaks lies, takes possession of someone else's goods, desires another man's wife, and who, being in a thirst for excitement, indulges in intoxicating drinks: he digs into his own root in this world.

O man! Know that death is prepared for you: watch yourself, so that self-interest and vanity do not draw you into untimely grief.

In the one for whom all envy has faded, in whom it is uprooted, he enjoys peace, day and night.

—Dhammapada

July 23 – Duty

The truly good deeds are those that are beneficial for all people.

—Marcus Aurelius

Love your God with all your heart. May your heart be wholly dedicated to God, may peace be established in your inner world, so that your sensual desires are completely subordinate to a sense of duty.

—Talmud

July 24 – Purity

"He who is not with me is against me; and whoever does not gather with me scatters."

—JESUS / LUKE 11:23

It is good when the body tires from mental activities, but it is bad when mental abilities suffer from pleasures of the body.

—TALMUD

Glory to the man who at the time of his death is as pure and innocent as at the time of his birth.

—TALMUD

July 25 – Entertainment

For the most part, people who spend their time in various troublesome activities imagine that as soon as they finish their work, they will indulge in a sweet rest right away. They do not understand that the passion for intense, frivolous activity is as insatiable as the need for entertainment, and it also stems from the fear of being left alone with yourself. These people think that they want to finish their work as soon as possible and find peace in relaxation, but in fact they are not looking for anything but excitement, passion and intoxication.

This is how the whole life of these people goes. With great effort, they overcome various obstacles in order to achieve the desired peace. But when this peace comes, it becomes unbearable for them: boredom comes from the depths of their souls and fills them with its poison.

—Blaise Pascal

July 26 - Truth

No truth leads to discouragement. The best proof of a just cause is that it has power over our hearts. It delights us, conquers us, and helps us.

—John Ruskin

To tell the truth is as good as to write well and is achieved only through practice; it is not so much a matter of will as of habit, and I do not think that any effort that helps the manifestation or formation of this habit could ever be considered useless.

—John Ruskin

July 27 - Anxiety

When I see a person who is tormenting himself with some fears and anxieties, I ask myself: what does this unfortunate person need? He probably wants something that is not in his power and which he cannot achieve by himself, because when what I want is in my power, I can't worry about it, but directly do what I want.

Look, for example, at a man singing or playing a harp: while he sings or plays for himself, without having any listeners, he does not worry, and he knows no fears or doubts. But look at him when he plays in front of a large crowd of people. How tormented he is, how pale and blushing he is, how much his heart beats! And why?

Because he wants not only to play and sing well, but also for people to praise him, and this, obviously, does not depend on him, but on his listeners. And so, he worries about what he cannot dispose of himself, and he torments himself completely in vain. He is not worried that he will not sing or play badly. No, he knows his job well; he is not worried about his work. He worries about the praise of the people, and this is not in his power.

When a person desires that which is not given to him, and turns away from what he cannot avoid, then his desires are not in order: he is ill with a desire disorder just as people are sick with an upset stomach and liver problem.

Any person who is worried about the future or torments himself with various anxieties and fears that do not depend on him is sick with desire.

—Epictetus

July 28 – Providence

The doctor prescribes one treatment for one patient, another for the other, but our Providence prescribes us illnesses, injuries and deplorable losses.

Just as the doctor's prescriptions tend to restore the patient's health, so our Providence leads a person towards moral improvement: to restore the connection of his troubled personal existence with the common life of all mankind.

So: take everything that falls to you as you will take the

doctor's medicines. Restoring the body's health is the point of these bitter medicines. After all, for the universal rational nature, the preservation of each creature's purpose is just as important as the patient's preservation of the health of the body.

Therefore, you need to welcome everything that happens to you, even the most bitter, because the meaning of such accidents is the health and integrity of the universe. Nature, living by its laws, acts reasonably, and everything that comes from it unerringly contributes to the preservation of unity.

—Marcus Aurelius

July 29 – Self-Knowledge

"Know thyself" is the basic rule. But do you really think that you can know yourself by peering into yourself? No, you can know yourself only by looking closely at what is outside of you. Compare your strengths with the strengths of others, your interests with their interests. Try to understand how you seem to them, and how they are to you, and judge yourself as someone else, based on the belief that you probably have nothing special.

—John Ruskin

If three of us converge, then I will probably find two teachers. I will try to imitate a kind person, and while observing a depraved person, I will try to correct myself.

—Chinese wisdom (Le-Lun-Yu)

July 30 - Truth

Truth is the beginning and end of everything that exists. If there were no truth, then there would be nothing. Therefore, the sages look at the truth as a treasure.

The truth not only exists in itself, but it also created all things. It exists by itself because it is love, it created things because it is wisdom and it is natural virtue and Tao—combining the external with the internal. Although people ignore the truth, it will never lose its meaning.

—Confucius

July 31 - Essence

If you do evil—you yourself suffer. When you yourself flee from sinfulness, you purify yourself from evil. You make yourself clean; no one else can do this for you.

—Dhammapada

Soul and flesh: this is what a person considers his own, about which he constantly cares. But know that you yourself, your essence, is in the spirit. Penetrate this consciousness, exalt your spirit above the flesh, preserve it from all worldly external dirt, do not let the flesh crush it, do not identify your life with the flesh, but merge with the life of your spirit, then you will fulfill all truth and live peacefully in the power of God, fulfilling his laws in this life.

—Marcus Aurelius

AUGUST

August 1 – Humility

He who seeks scholarship with meekness grows constantly in the eyes of the people of this world.

He who seeks reason becomes humbler every day.

He who becomes humbler diminishes himself until he reaches complete humility. When he achieves complete humility, there is nothing that he cannot accomplish.

—Lao-Tze

August 2 – Corollaries

True words are not pleasant; pleasant words are not true.

The good people are not those who argue; those who argue are not good.

The wise are not learned; the learned ones are not wise.

A holy man does not acquire riches for himself; the more he does for others, the more he gains.

The heavenly mind is beneficent and does no harm. The mind of a holy man makes him act but not argue.

—Lao-Tze

August 3 – Repetition

The following words were carved in King Ching Chang's bath: "Renew yourself completely every day: do it again, again, and again."

—Chinese wisdom (Ta-Hio)

The virtue of the sages reminds one of a journey to a distant land or an ascent to a great height; those who go to a distant land begin their walk from the first step and those ascending to a great height start from the bottom of the mountain.

—Confucius

August 4 – Solitude

In order not to spill a full vessel, you need to keep it carefully straight. To make the blade sharp, you need to constantly sharpen it. If gold and precious stones fill the house, it is difficult to preserve them. The rich, noble, and proud bring misfortune on themselves. In order to accomplish something and gain fame, it is best to retire into solitude.

This is the true path of holiness.

—Lao-Tze

How good it is for a person when he languishes in vain, searches for good in worldly life, and finally—getting tired of this—stretches out his hands to God.

—Blaise Pascal

August 5 – Corporality

We do not have enough knowledge to even understand the life of the human body. See what you need to know and what your body needs: the body needs a place, time, movement, warmth, light, food, water, air, and much more.

In nature, everything is so closely interconnected that one cannot know one without studying the other. One cannot know parts without knowing the whole. We will understand the life of our body only when we can study everything that it needs; and for this it is necessary to study the whole universe. But the universe is infinite, and its knowledge is unattainable for man. Therefore, we cannot fully understand the true life of our body.

—Blaise Pascal

August 6 – Eternity

A man is imprisoned and does not know whether his sentence has been passed on him. But in fact he has only one hour left. If he then finds out that he is sentenced to death, and that this hour is enough to procure the annulment of his sentence, is he really going to use this hour, not to find the means of procuring the annulment but to play cards? It would not be wise. People who do not think about God and eternity do precisely this.

—Blaise Pascal

Every bird knows where to make her home. Knowing where her home is, she knows her purpose in life. How can a person, the wisest of all beings, not know the same thing as a bird?

—Chinese wisdom (Ta-Hio)

August 7 - Hierarchy

"How many of you—having a servant plowing or looking after the sheep—will tell him when he returns from the field: 'Go quickly, sit down at the table.'

"On the contrary, will you not say to him: 'Prepare my supper, and get yourself ready to wait on me while I eat and drink. After that, you may then eat and drink yourself.'

"Will you thank the servant because he did what he was told to do?

"So, you also, when you have done everything you were told to do, should say, 'We are unworthy servants; we have only done our duty.'"

—Jesus / Luke 17:7–10

Take a place lower than befits you. This is better for you.

He who exalts himself is humiliated by God and he who humbles himself is exalted by God.

—Talmud

August 8 – Industry

Wise consumption is much more difficult than wise production. What twenty people can hardly produce, one can easily consume, and the question of life—both for each individual and for the whole nation—is not how much he could produce, but what these products are spent on.

People usually argue that personal practice is powerless to influence the change or delay of the vast system of modern industry or the methods of production and trade.

I—reflecting on the many clever conversations that enter one ear and leave through another without making the slightest impression on the mind—sometimes feel an irresistible desire to try and use all the rest of my life to silently do the thing that I think is reasonable and never talk about anything.

—John Ruskin

August 9 – Pleasure

Some people are so afraid of the ignorance in which they must live, so afraid of death and all sorts of misfortune, that they try not to think about these things at all.

They are constantly looking for new entertainment and pleasure, thinking thereby to drown their anxiety and gain happiness. In this way they cannot obtain satisfaction, since a person who seeks his pleasure is never satisfied. Having received what he wanted, he does not calm down, but at the same time experiences new desires that are not yet satisfied.

—Blaise Pascal

Usually people think that the king's life is the best life. However, if the king is left without entertainment and has time only to think about what he himself is, then he will see his unhappy position, remembering everything that threatens him: disobedience, unrest, illness, and death. And therefore, the king, if he is not enjoying himself, is more unhappy than his least subject: who is free to play cards and enjoy himself.

—Blaise Pascal

August 10 – Abundance

The heavenly mind acts like a person pulling a bow. He lowers what was above and lifts up what was lower. He takes away from those who have abundance and adds to those who have need. That is the heavenly mind. Yet, the human mind is not like that. We take from the poor to add to the abundant. Therefore, the holy man, having excess, gives it to the whole world.

—Lao-Tze

August 11 – Submission

It is unusual for a wise person to talk about the nature of creatures above or below him. It is too immodest. To recognize his eternal relative greatness and insignificance, to know himself and his place in nature, to be content with his submission to God, while not being able to comprehend it, and to control the lower creatures with love and kindness without sharing their animal passions and not imitating them—this is what it means to be humble in relation to God, kind to his creatures and wise to himself.

—John Ruskin

August 12 – Reaping

One of the specific conditions of human labor is that completeness is in the moment between the time of sowing and reaping, and because the goal of our aspirations is in general very remote, the less we want to see the fruits of our labors, the greater and broader will be the measure of our success.

—John Ruskin

One who creates evil flourishes until the fruit of his evil deed has ripened; but when this fruit ripens, then he will see all the evil he has done.

When the virtuous person sees evil, he thinks that the fruits of his good deeds have not yet ripened, and he will be blessed when his good deeds bear good fruit.

—Dhammapada

August 13 – Castigation

Do not seek glory in the disgrace of others.

It is appropriate for an enlightened man to hide the shame of others, even those who have harmed him.

Do not remind the penitent of his past transgressions.

—Talmud

August 14 – Enemies

"But I tell you: love your enemies, bless those who curse you, do good to those who hate you, and pray for those who offend and persecute you."

—Jesus / Matthew 5:44

A wonderful quality in a man is the ability to love those who oppose him. This love is awakened in him by understanding the fact that all people are brothers, that they err against their will, that both the offender and the victim will face the same end and, most importantly, that the offence cannot harm a person because only he himself can harm his soul.

—Marcus Aurelius

August 15 – Tranquility

"Here I will dwell during the rains; there I will settle down in the summer." Thus, the madman dreams and does not think about death, but death comes suddenly and carries away a man preoccupied, selfish, and scattered, and it happens like a flood washes away a sleeping village.

Neither son, nor father, nor relatives, nor friends: no one will help us when death strikes us. The good and wise, having clearly realized the meaning of this, will quickly clear the path leading to tranquility.

—Dhammapada

August 16 – Change

Are you afraid of change? Think of this: nothing in the world is done without change. The very essence of universal nature is change. It is impossible to warm the water without burning wood; nutrition is impossible without being able to cook.

All worldly life is nothing but change. Understand that the transformation awaiting you is exactly the same, that it is made necessary by the very nature of things. It is necessary to take care of one thing, so as not to do something contrary to the true nature of humanity: to act in everything, as and when it is indicated.

—Marcus Aurelius

August 17 – Simplicity

Every true science begins with love, and not when we analyze our brothers; and it ends with love, and not when we try to analyze God.

—John Ruskin

The sage said: my teaching is simple, and its meaning is easy to understand. It consists of loving your neighbor as you love yourself.

—Chinese wisdom (Le-Lun-Yu)

August 18 – Genius

It has already been stated more than once, and quite rightly, that the whole difference between a genius and other people is that a genius, for the most part, remains a child looking into the world with wide eyes, full of endless wonder at his awareness, not of his great significance, but his infinite ignorance, and at the same time his power.

—John Ruskin

When people study for themselves, then the teaching process is good for them, but when people do it with the purpose to look like scholars, then the learning is useless.

—Chinese wisdom (Le-Lun-Yu)

August 19 – Commandments

Son of man! Do not listen to the whisper of the tempter who will tell you to think: "Am I made of stone? Unless my flesh is of copper, then you are laying this heavy burden on me—fulfilling the commandments. All my days and my nights will not be enough to fulfill all this." Know that such thoughts are the whispers of an evil tempter, who presents you with the commandments that are difficult to fulfill so that you will deviate from the truth and fall into the trap. Know also that more than half of the commandments are prohibitions, telling a person only "do not". Again, the rest are the commandments about the unity of God and constant love for him, that you do not harm your neighbor, stay away from robbery, etc. Thus, the commandments are very easy to fulfill, since most of them are passive, that is, requiring only abstinence from action.

—Talmud

August 20 - Aid

Consider all your talents and knowledge as the means you have to help others.

The strong and wise man was given his gifts not to oppress, but to help others and support the weak.

—John Ruskin

August 21 - Heroism

"You heard what is said: Love your neighbor and hate your enemy. But I tell you: love your enemies, and pray for those who persecute you."

—Jesus / Matthew 5:43–44

Who is the hero? He who is turning his enemy into a friend.

—Talmud

August 22 - Mistakes

Honest enthusiastic mistakes are never harmful, because they are always made in the right direction and fall in front along the road, not in the moat behind, and therefore can be corrected by the person following.

—John Ruskin

The mistakes of a wise man are like the eclipses of the sun and moon. When he is mistaken, all people see this and also see how he corrected himself.

—Chinese wisdom (Le-Lun-Yu)

August 23 – Ignorance

Smug and gross ignorance will produce an imperfect but harmless person. Ignorance is displeased and cunning, studying what it is not able to understand and imitating what it cannot enjoy, producing the most disgusting, humiliating and corrupting humanity.

—John Ruskin

August 24 – Competition

Throw nuts and gingerbread cookies on the street and immediately the children will come running. They will pick them up, and they will fight among themselves. Adults will not fight in such a situation. And when you throw out empty shells, the children will not pick them up.

For me, money, positions, honors and fame are the same as shells and children's sweets. Let the children pick them up, let them fight one another because of this, let them kiss the hands of the rich dignitaries and their minions. For me, it's all shells. If by chance a nut falls into my hands, why not eat it? But to bend down in order to pick it up, to fight because of it, to knock someone off their feet or to fall down yourself, it is not worth it for such trifles.

—Epictetus

August 25 – Folly

The older a spiritual person becomes, the more his mental horizons expand, the more his consciousness becomes clearer, while an ignoramus becomes ever more ignorant over the years.

—TALMUD

A wise person constantly grows in reason and discernment, but a thoughtless person constantly falls into ignorance and vice.

—CHINESE WISDOM (LE-LUN-YU)

August 26 – Tenderness

The weakest in the world can defeat the strongest. Therefore, there is a great advantage in humility and a benefit in silence. Only a few in the world can be humble.

—LAO-TZE

Man, when he lives, is gentle and flexible. When he dies, he becomes hard and dry. All things, like grass and trees, are gentle and flexible while they live. When they die, they are made brittle and dry. Therefore, hard and strong are death's companions. Soft and tender are life's partners. One who is strong with his physical strength only, will not win. When the tree became strong, it was doomed to death. Strong and large are at the bottom, tender and soft at the top.

—LAO-TZE

August 27 – Virtues

The reward for the fulfillment of the commandments is a commandment; that is, if someone obeys only one of the commandments, then the Lord opens up the possibility for him to fulfill the others, which is an important reward, because this leads to his own benefit.

—TALMUD

No virtue is ever alone. It always has other virtues as its neighbors.

—CHINESE WISDOM (LE-LUN-YU)

August 28 – Tomorrow

"Therefore, I say to you: do not care what you should eat or drink or wear. Is life not more than food or clothes?

"Take a look at the birds of the air: they neither sow, nor reap, nor store away in the granary and yet your heavenly father feeds them. Are you not more valuable then they?

"Can any one of you by worrying add a single hour to your life?

"So, do not worry and do not say, 'What do we have?' or 'what do we drink?' or 'what do we wear?'

"Seek first the kingdom of God and his truth, and all this will be added to you.

"So, do not worry about tomorrow, because tomorrow itself will take care of its own; it is enough to care for each day."

—JESUS / MATTHEW 6:25–27, 31, 33–34

Who, having bread in a basket, asks: what will I eat tomorrow? This question is asked by the faithless.

—Talmud

August 29 – Pleasure

Out of pleasure, sadness arises; out of pleasure, fear arises. Whoever is free from pleasure, for him there is no sorrow or fear.

—Dhammapada

People seek pleasure, rushing from place to place only because they feel the emptiness of their life, but they do not yet feel the emptiness of the new pleasures that attract them.

—Blaise Pascal

August 30 – Fears

Whoever is afraid of God is not afraid of people. And whoever is afraid of people is not afraid of God.

To please all, this is the same as to carry water in a sieve.

—Proverbs

August 31 – Butterflies

Do not be afraid of ignorance, be afraid of false knowledge. From it comes all the evil of the world.

—Leo Tolstoy

It is a misfortune for people when they do not know God, but it is even worse when they seem to recognize in God something that is not God.

—Lucius Lactantius

Great thoughts come from the heart.

—Marquis de Vauvenargues

People who think that it is all about knowledge are like those moths that fly to candles; they themselves die and obscure the light.

—Leo Tolstoy

SEPTEMBER

September 1 – Peace of Mind

Some say, "Enter, and you will find peace." This is not the whole truth.

Others, on the contrary, say, "Get out of yourself; try to forget yourself and you will find happiness in entertainment." This is unfair, if only because it is impossible to get rid of, for example, diseases in this way.

Peace and happiness are neither within us, nor outside of us; they are in God who is both inside and outside of us.

—Blaise Pascal

September 2 – Temptation

The human soul is subject to several temptations against which you must always be ready to fight. One is castle-building—restrain it by saying to yourself, "That which I am thinking at the present moment is idle." Another is lying—"What I am going to say will be against my conscience, and therefore against the truth." Finally, the feeling of voluptuousness—suppress it with the consciousness that you are doing irreparable harm to your divine principle by unbridling the flesh, and helping your blind instinctive nature to become higher than your spiritual essence.

—Marcus Aurelius

September 3 – Mutual Aid

A person increases his happiness to the extent that he delivers it to others.

—Jeremy Bentham

The will of God is that we live in happiness with the lives of others, and not with mutual misfortune. People help each other with their joy, not grief.

—John Ruskin

September 4 – Evil

"For out of the heart come evil thoughts—murder, sexual immorality, theft, false testimony, and slander."

—Jesus / Matthew 15:19

Actions are not as kind or perverse as our desires.

—Marquis de Vauvenargues

In the distance are immoral thoughts. They quietly sneak in, remaining deeply hidden; he who subjugates them to himself, who restrains them, will be freed from their temptation.

—Dhammapada

September 5 – Truth

Truth is like a circle: she is able to clothe herself with form. When she is clothed with form, she is revealed. The revealed truth is obvious to everyone. The obvious then brings about change, and such change brings about conversion. Truth can transform the world.

—Confucius

September 6 – Estrangement

A skilled military man is not warlike. A skilled fighter is never angry. One who is skilled in leading people is humble. This is called the virtue of non-resistance. It is reconciliation with heaven.

—Lao-Tze

The branch that is cut off from its trunk is thereby separated from the whole tree. A man in contention with another person breaks away from all of humanity, for he has unwittingly cut off a human branch, and unknowingly alienated himself from his neighbor with hatred and anger.

—Marcus Aurelius

September 7 – Giving

The virtue of philanthropy is not far from us. You only want to practice philanthropy, and it will come to you.

Be strict with yourself and lenient with others, and you will not have enemies.

—Chinese wisdom (Le-Lun-Yu)

September 8 – Humility

The first distinguishing feature of a kind and wise person is the consciousness that he knows very little, that there are many people who are much more learned than he is. He always wants to know and learn, not teach.

Those who struggle to teach or manage can neither teach nor manage well.

—John Ruskin

September 9 – Forbearance

My flesh is subject to all kinds of external calamities and sufferings. Let the flesh complain if it is harmed. But as long as I don't acknowledge with my mind that which happened to the flesh, my essence will remain unharmed.

Do not be rash. Bear your burden. Let it serve you for good. Take from it what is needed for your intelligent life, as the stomach extracts from food everything that is needed for the flesh, or like a fire that flares up brighter when fuel is fed into it.

—Marcus Aurelius

September 10 – Resolve

In the morning, you need to take care of yourself and say to yourself, "I can now come into conflict with a person who is impudent, ungrateful, arrogant, hypocritical, bothersome or embittered, because everyone who does not know what is good and what is bad is filled with such vices. But if I myself firmly know what good and evil are, I understand that evil for me is only an evil deed that I myself do, and then no offender can harm me, for no one can force me, against my will, to do evil."

—MARCUS AURELIUS

September 11 – Steadfastness

"The one who stands firm to the end will be saved."

—JESUS / MATTHEW 24:13

Glory be given to the man who does not give in to temptation. For God sees everyone's experiences, rich and poor alike. He will open his hand to the needy and the poor.

—TALMUD

That which we call happiness and that which we call misfortune are equally useful to us if we look at both as a test.

—LEO TOLSTOY

September 12 – Baseness

The lowest of all the provisions of knowledge to which modern sirens point is their attempt to find a different source of life than love.

—JOHN RUSKIN

While people sentimentally preach the commandment, "Love one's neighbor as oneself," in fact they often behave like wild animals, clutching these neighbors in their claws, trampling them underfoot. In actuality, many can live by the labors of others.

—John Ruskin

September 13 – Piety

Piety always begins with modesty. You must first feel that you are insignificant, and therefore you should listen to what you are told. Then think about what you are told and who tells you, and you will find that you always have a clear concept of good and evil that you can follow.

—John Ruskin

September 14 – Repentance

Whoever says, "I will sin and I will repent," will find that he cannot repent. He who says: "I will sin and the day of repentance will atone for my sins": that day of repentance does not atone for his sin.

The deeds of repentance redeem the deeds in relation to God; but the day of repentance does not atone for the misconduct, until the neighbor is satisfied.

—Talmud

Repentance is only valid when a person abstains from that of which he repented.

—Leo Tolstoy

September 15 – Holiness

The seas rule over all the valleys through which the rivers

flow because the seas are lower than the valleys.

Therefore, a holy man, if he wants to be above the people, must be lower than them in his speeches. If he wants to lead them, then he must be behind them.

Therefore, a holy man lives above the people, but the people do not feel this. He is in front of the people, but the people do not suffer from this. Therefore, the world, without ceasing, praises him. Since he does not argue with anyone, no one in the world argues with him.

—Lao-Tze

September 16 – Judas

We are extremely unfair to Judas Iscariot, considering him a terribly bad man. For how many such lovers of money do you think there are who would hang themselves out of compassion for anyone executed because of them?

—John Ruskin

September 17 – Wisdom

The wise man was asked: "What is the outstanding virtue of humanity?" He answered: "It is to love people."

He was also asked: "What is science?" He said: "To know people."

—Chinese wisdom (Le-Lun-Yu)

The sage respects three things: he respects the laws of heaven, respects noble people, and respects the words of saints. Ignorant people do not know the laws of heaven, and therefore do not respect them, they do not value noble people, and they laugh at the words of the saints.

—Chinese wisdom (Le-Lun-Yu)

September 18 – Righteousness

"Not everyone who says to me, 'Lord, Lord!' will enter the kingdom of heaven, but only the one who does the will of my Father who is in heaven."

—Jesus / Matthew 7:21

One who knows the rules of common sense is lower than the one who loves them, and the one who loves them is lower than the one who performs them.

—Chinese wisdom (Le-Lun-Yu)

September 19 – Revelation

When rainwater flows through the gutters, it seems to us that it flows out of them, whereas in reality it falls from the sky. It is the same with the holy teachings that good people give us. It seems that they come from them, but they really come from God.

—Brahmin's wisdom (Ramakrishna)

In order to take out a needle that is embedded in a leg, take another to extract it; when this is done, then throw out both one and the other. Similarly, the mind needs only to eliminate the madness that obscures the vision of the divine, but truly neither the mind nor the madness can lead to true revelation. One who has attained true revelation cannot be called either intelligent or mad, because he is freed from all duality.

—Brahmin's wisdom (Ramakrishna)

September 20 - Service

There are people who, having done someone a favor, immediately consider themselves entitled to expect a reward for it. Others, not counting on a direct reward, do not forget the service rendered and in their hearts acknowledge that they have debtors. Finally, there are those who are always ready to serve, almost involuntarily. These people are like a vine, which having produced its fruit, is quite satisfied that it alone ripened its characteristic fruit.

—Marcus Aurelius

September 21 - Abstinence

Abstinence does not mean suppression or underdevelopment of energy. It does not mean suspension in goodness, such as in the manifestation of love or faith. On the contrary, it is the strength and energy that prevents doing what a person considers bad.

—John Ruskin

A man who achieves virtue, even if he is not intelligent, is firm in his actions. He may be weak in body, but strong in spirit.

—Confucius

September 22 – Miscellany

Your enemy will repay evil, the hater will painfully repay evil, but the incomparably burning evil will bring you an erring mind.

Neither father nor mother nor relatives will do you so much good as your mind when it has chosen the right path.

—DHAMMAPADA

Some easily do good deeds. Others do them with the help of various devices. And, finally, others do them through many works. All, nonetheless, perform good deeds.

—CONFUCIUS

September 23 – Purity

Knowledge is food for the mind, just as there is food for the body. It is, therefore, subject to the same abuse as physical food. It can be mixed and adulterated so that it becomes unhealthy. It can be refined and sweetened, so that it loses all nutritional value. And even the best mental food can be infected so that you end with disease and even death.

—JOHN RUSKIN

September 24 – Joy

Go and see the difference between earthly and divine things. In the earthly things only an empty vessel is filled, while in the divine the heart is filled. Full hearts are already imbued with divine things, and can perceive a new teaching, while empty hearts remain deaf to it.

—Talmud

You will find peace for your soul if you take the yoke of Christ upon yourself, but you will find joy only when you carry this yoke for as long as it is required. Only then will you truly enter into the joy of your master.

—John Ruskin

September 25 – Finding God

"Very truly I tell you, no one can see the kingdom of God unless they are born again."

—Jesus / John 3:3

The light of reason, born of moral perfection, is called natural virtue. Moral perfection, born of the light of reason, is called acquired holiness. They depend on each other.

—Chinese wisdom (Chung-Jung)

Love and reason are the two lenses through which we can contemplate God.

—Leo Tolstoy

September 26 – Delusion

Understand well and remember that a person always does what he thinks is best for himself. If something is actually better for him, then he is right; if he is mistaken, then it is worse for him. For after delusion suffering necessarily follows.

If you constantly remember this, then you will neither become angry nor indignant at anyone. You will neither reproach nor scold anyone, and you will not be at odds with anyone.

—Epictetus

September 27 – Self-Awareness

"Know thyself" is the basic rule. But do you really think that you can know yourself by peering into yourself? No, you can know yourself only by looking closely at what is outside of you. Compare your strengths with the strengths of others, your interests with their interests, try to understand how you seem to them and how they are to you. Judge yourself as something secondary, based on the belief that there is probably nothing special in you.

—John Ruskin

September 28 – Divinity

Love is not the main beginning of our life. Love is a consequence, not a cause. The reason for love is the consciousness in oneself of the divine spiritual principle. This consciousness requires love. It produces love.

—Leo Tolstoy

Life is that which is revealed through consciousness. It is omnipresent. Our misconception is that what closes life to us, we recognize as life.

—LEO TOLSTOY

September 29 - Multiplicity

The work is well done only when it is done with pleasure, but not a single person can willingly work if he is not aware that he is doing exactly what is needed at this moment.

In the eyes of the creator of everything great and small, the most insignificant thing has the same meaning as the greatest. The day, like thousands of years, and all the most insignificant, like the greatest, are full of the inexplicable mystery of the great spirit.

—JOHN RUSKIN

It would be most useful to write a description of the lives of those people about whom the world had not thought and heard, but who now carry out the main share of all his works, and from whom we can best learn how to perform them.

—JOHN RUSKIN

September 30 - Righteousness

The works of the righteous are seeds that sometimes lie motionless in the soil of history for a long time. But having received heat and moisture, having absorbed new, healthy juices and fresh forces, they begin to grow, blossom, and bear fruit. On the contrary, seeds sown by violence and unrighteousness rot, wither, and disappear without a trace.

—Talmud

Every generation should honor its distinguished people but do not say: "Their predecessors were worthier."

—Talmud

OCTOBER

October 1 – Virtue

A man of the highest virtue tries to follow the straight path to the end. Walking only half your distance is of no value. It's something to fear.

—Chinese wisdom (Chung-Jung)

Virtue in a man must have the property of a gem that invariably preserves its natural beauty, no matter what happens to it.

—Marcus Aurelius

October 2 – Goals

"Very truly I tell you, my Father will give you whatever you ask in my name."

—Jesus / John 16:23

With desire and ambition, there is no simple and virtuous act of which a person would not be capable.

—Chinese wisdom (Le-Lun-Yu)

October 3 – Passions

I would like to encourage people to seek the truth so they may free themselves from their passions that prevent them from going where they can find the truth. I know how passion and lust obscure understanding, and I would like a person to hate in himself all these carnal properties that blind him when he chooses his path and stop him when he already pursues his ambitions.

—Blaise Pascal

When a person clearly recognizes the place where he should stay forever, his inner self is determined. When his inner self is determined, all excessive excitement will cease. When such excitement ceases, there will be complete peace of mind, and a person who has unbreakable peace of mind will be capable of incredible mental activity. Such a person can find true wisdom.

—Confucius

October 4 – Sagacity

One who knows does not speak. One who speaks does not know. Therefore, the sage keeps his mouth closed and the gates of his feelings shut. He blunts his sharpness, unties his knots, and softens his radiance.

Thus, he is inaccessible to lust and hostility, to profit and loss, and he is as inaccessible to success as he is to shame. He is therefore revered by the whole world.

—Lao-Tze

October 5 – Knowledge

I learned much from my mentors, even more from my friends, and most of all from my students.

—Talmud

When you see a sage, think about whether you have the same virtues as him. When you see a libertine, think about whether you have the same vices.

—Chinese wisdom (Le-Lun-Yu)

October 6 – Reverence

Know that we pray to God and submit our requests to him, not because his will is subject to change, but because our begging satisfies our needs. We thereby acknowledge that he created the world, that he cares for everyone, and dominates all that he oversees—all affairs, both good and bad—and, recognizing the glory of the Lord and all his power, our soul is all the while purified.

—Talmud

October 7 – The Path

The law of Heaven is perfect, without any flaws. Perfection, that is the use of all one's forces to know the law of Heaven, is the law of man. He who constantly strives for his perfection is a wise man who knows how to distinguish good from evil. He chooses the good and clings firmly to it, so as never to lose it.

—Chinese wisdom (Chung-Jung)

No matter how little I am educated, I can always follow the path of the mind. One thing I need to fear is conceit. To achieve the higher mind is very simple, yet people do not like the straight path but the short cuts.

—Lao-Tze

October 8 – Resolve

A wise person is firm in his decisions, never entering into a clash with other people. Not belonging to the crowd, such a person lives in peace with it.

—Chinese wisdom (Le-Lun-Yu)

If someone offended me, it is his business. Such is his inclination; such is his disposition. I have my own temperament, as I was given by nature, and I will remain faithful to that nature in my actions.

—Marcus Aurelius

October 9 – Obedience

"Anyone who chooses to do the will of God will find out whether my teaching comes from God or whether I speak from myself."

—Jesus / John 7:17

The whole of history confirms the indisputable fact that God can be understood not by reason, but by obedience. The presence of eternal order in the world becomes apparent only when the commandments of God are fulfilled. Only in this way can we know his will on earth.

There are known eternal laws for human life that are quite easily demonstrable by the human mind. And the more people understand these laws and follow them, the more strength and virtue they will have to live their lives.

—John Ruskin

October 10 - Roots

"A good man brings good things out of the good stored up in him, and an evil man brings evil things out of the evil stored up in him."

—Jesus / Matthew 12:35

What is likened to one whose wisdom prevails over his deeds? A tree with many branches but small roots: the first wind that comes will rip it out and upset it. And what is likened to the one whose affairs prevail over his wisdom? A tree with few branches, but deep roots: all the winds of the world will not budge it.

—Talmud

Pious people promise little and do a lot; evil people promise a lot, but do little.

—Talmud

October 11 - Spirit

Wherever fate throws you, everywhere your essence will follow you. It is your spirit, the focus of life, freedom and strength, which is faithful to the law of its being. There are no external goods or greatness in the world for which a person should break his unity with his spirit, terminate his union with it, or undermine the integrity of his soul with internal discord.

What could you buy at the cost of such a sacrifice?

—Marcus Aurelius

October 12 – Priorities

They asked the sage, "What time in life is the most important? Which person is the most important? And what is the most important thing?"

And the sage replied thusly: "The present time is the most important, because in it a man has power over himself. The most important person is the one you are dealing with at this present moment, because no one can know if he will not soon be dealing with other persons. And the most important thing is to be in love with this person, because that is the sole purpose for which a person is sent into life."

—Leo Tolstoy

October 13 – Collusion

The mistake of all good people in our time is that while they politely hold out their hand to the evil people and support them in their evil deeds, they hope to avert the consequence of evil, working to correct the harm done to them.

In the morning, in order to satisfy their hearts' needs, they help the needs of two or three devastated families. But in the evening they dine with the destroyers of these families, envy them, and prepare to follow the example of a rich speculator who ruined the lives of two or three thousand people. Thus, they destroy in a few hours more than they can fix for decades, or at best, in vain they feed the starving population in the wake of an all-consuming army, which they are trying to increase in size and speed.

—John Ruskin

October 14 - Cain

There are very few people who really want to do evil. In fact, there may not be any at all. Evildoers simply do not know what they are doing. Cain, killing Abel, did not think he was doing anything wrong. Among us there are countless Cains who kill their brothers daily, all the while not thinking that they are doing wrong. The whole difficulty is to open their eyes. Affecting their feelings and affecting their hearts is not difficult, but it is not easy to influence their minds. You cannot always be at their fingertips to point out to them what is fair, and so they will easily begin to act just as unjustly, and perhaps even worse than before. People often say that hell is paved with good intentions, but this is not true. You cannot pave the bottomless abyss; you can only pave the way.

—John Ruskin

October 15 - Truth

No matter how hard you try, it is very difficult to constantly do what is good. No matter how many good things you do, you will always have the desire to do more.

—Confucius

Invariably, speaking the truth is almost as difficult, and perhaps as valiant, as living the truth, despite threats and punishments. It is strange that, for the vast number of people who defend the truth at the cost of their wealth, at the cost of their lives, there are so few who defend it at the cost of a little daily anxiety.

—John Ruskin

October 16 – Worship

True worship is free from superstition; when superstition enters, worship collapses. Christ showed us what true worship is. He taught that of all that we do in our life, one thing is the light and happiness of all people: our love for each other. He taught that we can achieve our happiness only when we serve people, not ourselves.

—Blaise Pascal

October 17 – Estrangement

"If they persecuted me, they will persecute you also. If they obeyed my teaching, they will obey yours also. They will treat you this way because of my name, for they do not know the one who sent me."

—Jesus / John 15:20–21

To be unknown to people or not to be understood by them and not to grieve about this is the characteristic of a truly virtuous person.

—Chinese wisdom (Le-Lun-Yu)

"Let the fear of heaven be as strong in people as the fear of humans." Oh, if only it were! After all, when a person commits a crime, he only thinks, "No matter what, I don't want people to see me."

—Talmud

October 18 - Miscellany

Humans are by nature direct. If this natural directness is lost during life, then a person cannot be happy.

—Chinese wisdom (Le-Lun-Yu)

If we are sitting on a moving ship and looking at some object on the same ship, then our movement is invisible to us; if we look to the side at an object that does not move with us, for example, to the shore, then we will immediately notice our movement. The same thing happens in life. When all people do not live as they should, it is imperceptible. When a person comes to his senses and heals himself according to God's will, only then will it immediately becomes obvious how the others act badly.

—Blaise Pascal

Despising all the good that is in great people, the world chooses only that which can produce evil, and thus spoils, perverts, nullifies, and even harms all the powers of the greatest people.

—John Ruskin

October 19 - Comprehension

Each word has only that meaning its listener can perceive. Therefore, you do not explain the meaning of honor to a dishonorable person, or the meaning of love to someone who is alien to it. Trying to reduce the meaning of these words to their understanding, you will only reach the point where you will no longer have words for the expression of honor and love.

—John Ruskin

October 20 - Hindrances

Beware of people who discourage you from striving to do good on the basis that perfection is utopia.

Never consider it futile to submit to an influence that can arouse noble feelings in you.

—John Ruskin

October 21 - Holiness

A holy man has no feelings of his own. The feelings of the people become his feelings. He meets the good with kindness, and he also meets the evil with kindness. He meets the faithful with faith, and with the same faith he meets the unbelievers.

A holy man, living in peace, is preoccupied with his relationship to people. He feels for all people, and all people turn their ears and eyes to him.

—Lao-Tze

October 22 – Searching

There are only three categories of people: some have found a god and serve him; these people are intelligent and happy. Others have not found him and are not looking for him; these people are ignorant and unhappy. Still others have not found him but seek him; these people are intelligent but still unhappy.

—Blaise Pascal

Where the search for truth begins, life always begins; as soon as the search for truth ceases, life also ceases.

—John Ruskin

October 23 – Purity

There are people who, as soon as they listen to wise teachings, they themselves begin to teach others. They do the same thing as a sick stomach, which instantly spews out ingested food. Do not imitate such people. First, digest in yourself what you heard, and do not spew out ahead of time—otherwise, vomit will come out that cannot serve as anyone's food.

—Epictetus

To achieve moral perfection, you must first take care of spiritual purity. And spiritual purity is achieved only when the heart seeks truth and the will strives for holiness. But all of this depends on true knowledge.

—Confucius

October 24 – Motivations

There are three engines of human life: the first is a feeling arising from various human interactions with other beings; the second is imitation and suggestion, and the third is the conclusions of the mind.

For a million acts committed as a result of the first two engines, hardly one is committed on the basis of the arguments of the mind. This distribution occurs both in individuals who undertake millions of acts and perform only one according to reason—and in different groups of people, where the people perform millions of acts and only one according to reason.

—Leo Tolstoy

October 25 – Faith

God instills faith in the heart of man through conscience and reason. It is impossible to instill faith by force and threats; force and threats do not instill faith, but horror. Unbelievers and those who are mistaken should not be condemned and reproached: they are already unhappy enough from their delusions. They should be reproached only if it could benefit them. But normally it only repels them, and causes them harm.

—Blaise Pascal

Do not think that someday you may be hurt by the efforts to penetrate other people's faith and mentally sympathize with the guiding principles of their lives. Only in this way can you justly love and appreciate them.

—John Ruskin

October 26 – Eternity

If you want to get used to thinking about death without fear, then try to peer into and enter the position of those people who were committed to life with all their might. It seemed to them that death befell them prematurely. Meanwhile, those who have lived the longest, having buried many, finally died. How short this period of time is! How much grief, evil, and fragility the vessel of life fits into itself! Is it worth talking about this moment? Think of this—eternity is behind you, eternity is ahead. Between these two abysses, what does it matter to you? Will you live for three days or three centuries?

—Marcus Aurelius

October 27 – Science

How strange it is to think that physical science should have been thought to be hostile to religion. Yet the pride of physical science is like every other pride, hostile to religion and truth. True science, however, is not only not hostile to religion, but also paves a path in the mountains for those who are going to look upon the world.

—John Ruskin

To know that you know what you know and to know that you do not know what you do not know is true science.

—Chinese wisdom (Le-Lun-Yu)

It would be better not to be born to someone who hopes to lift the veil from what is higher and lower than us, to see what happened before and what will happen after.

—Talmud

October 28 – Mercy

Just as the first rule of wisdom is to know one's self, although this is the most difficult thing, the first rule of mercy is to be content with one's self, although this is also difficult. Only such a contented and peaceful person will appear forceful and strong enough always to show mercy to others.

—John Ruskin

When true morality becomes clear, then everything else will be clear.

—Confucius

October 29 – Progress

Since you can find beings above you who you can look to with a sense of reverence or even deep reverence, so can you become nobler and happier. If you could always live among the archangels, you would be happier than in a society of people. And vice versa, if you were condemned to live in a crowd of idiots—dumb, ugly, evil creatures—you would not be happy with the eternal consciousness of your superiority. Thus, all the real joy and power of human progress depends on the fact that people find a worthy object of worship, and all the baseness in humanity begins with the habit of despising everything.

—John Ruskin

October 30 - Secrecy

Whenever something inherent in you is worthy of reproach, hurry to declare it to yourself.

—Talmud

In the actual practice of everyday life, you will find that wherever there is secrecy, there is crime or danger. It is, thus, unthinkable that there should be things that need secrecy, but, on the contrary, the dignity and safety of human life are directly dependent on its frankness.

—John Ruskin

October 31 - Savings

"Do not store up for yourselves treasures on earth, where moths and vermin destroy, and where thieves break in and steal. Store up for yourselves treasures in heaven, where moths and vermin do not destroy, and where thieves do not break in and steal. For where your treasure is, there your heart will be also."

—Jesus / Matthew 6:19–21

Gain for yourself the wealth that thieves cannot steal, that tyrants dare not encroach on, which will remain with you even after death, never to be diminished.

—Indian proverb

NOVEMBER

November 1 – Prayer

Prayer for any honest person is a clarification of his relationship to his creator: doing good to him every minute; the elucidation of his connection with people, his duties to them, as to the children of the same father; and settling accounts for all his actions; and also discussing his past in order to protect himself from future mistakes and misconduct that he fell into in the past.

—Talmud

November 2 – Fate

If you force the circumstances, you will see that the circumstances will be against you; and if you choose to yield to the circumstances, they will yield to you in return.

When you see that circumstances do not favor you, then do not resist them, but leave them to their natural course, because whoever goes against the circumstances becomes their slave, and whoever obeys them becomes their master.

—Talmud

There is no chance in fate; man creates rather than meets his fate.

—Abel-François Villemain

November 3 – Knowledge

Knowledge is like a golden coin. A person has the right to be proud of owning it if he himself worked on its gold and minted it, or at least honestly acquired it. But when he did not do this but received it from a passerby who threw it in his face, then what reason has he to be proud of it?

—John Ruskin

November 4 – Freedom

Only about someone who lives as he wants can we say that he is free: an intelligent man always lives as he wants, and no one in the world can stop him from doing this because he only wants what he can obtain. And therefore, a rational person is free.

No one wants to be guilty, no one wants to live in error, no one chooses on purpose a life that will cause him to grieve and suffer, no one will say that he wants to live badly and lewdly. This means that all people living an unrighteous life do not live like this according to their will but against their will. They want neither sadness nor fear, but meanwhile they constantly suffer and fear. They do what they do not want. Therefore, they are not free.

—Epictetus

November 5 – Prayer

Before you begin a prayer, test yourself on whether you

are able reverently to concentrate your thoughts. If you cannot, do not pray.

—Talmud

Prayer should not be started either under the influence of sadness or under the influence of laziness, laughter, chatter, frivolity, and idle conversation, but only under the influence of pious delight. If you are not in a good mood, it is better to refrain from prayer. He who makes prayer a habit, his prayer is not sincere.

—Talmud

November 6 – Justice

The only divine work, the only sacrificial commandment is justice, and we are least inclined to fulfill it. Demand from us anything but justice.

"But mercy," you say, "is exalted over judgment." Yes, this is true justice, it is its peak, it is a temple, the basis of justice. But you cannot reach the top without starting from the bottom. You can base your deeds not on mercy, but only on justice because there is no mercy without justice. She is the last reward for a good deed.

—John Ruskin

November 7 – Direction

"Come in at the narrow gate; for wide is the gate and broad is the way that leads to destruction, and many enter through it. But small is the gate and narrow the road that leads to life, and few find it."

—JESUS / MATTHEW 7:13–14

Thousands of paths lead to error; to truth—only one.

—JEAN-JACQUES ROUSSEAU

November 8 – Misfortune

When something upsets and torments you, think, first of all, how much worse could happen to you and happens to other people; second, remember how in the past you were upset and tormented by such events or circumstances that you now remember calmly and indifferently; and third, most importantly, think that what upsets and torments you is only a test for which you can show your faith and strengthen it.

—LAO-TZE

November 9 – Frivolity

Reflection is the path to immortality; thoughtlessness is the path to death. Awaken yourself and then protect yourself by vigorously reflecting on your life's direction, and you will invariably be made happy.

—DHAMMAPADA

Understand, finally, that in you there is a divine soul, standing above passions, cowardice, and confusion by which you are distorted, like a booth doll.

—MARCUS AURELIUS

November 10 - Justice

You push a person into a pit and then tell him that he should be satisfied with the position that his actions have placed him in. This is our modern Christianity. You say, "We didn't push this person into an abyss." Yes, of course, we will not be aware of all that we do—until every morning you start asking yourself the question, "How can you do during the day the things that are not profitable, but what is fair?" Then, one day, you would become a good Christian who could recognize the validity of the words of Mohammed: "An hour of justice is worth more than seventy years of prayer."

—John Ruskin

November 11 - Death

No one knows what death is and whether it is the greatest good for man. However, everyone is afraid of it, as if we understand that it is the greatest evil.

—Plato

It is equally unworthy of a rational man to desire death and also fear it.

—Arabic proverb

November 12 - Liberation

Who in his transient life, in his name and in his flesh, does not see himself, he knows the truth of life.

—Dhammapada

The words of the doctrine are strong only for those who deny their personality.

—Talmud

More glorious domination of the earth, more beautiful ascension to heaven, more glorious dominion of the worlds—the holy joy of the first stages of liberation.

—Dhammapada

November 13 - Grace

Leave your holiness and your prudence, and the people will be a hundred times happier. Leave your good nature and your justice, and the people will return to their former love between children and parents. Leave your cunning and your calculations, and there will be no more thieves and robbers. These three things cannot be achieved by one action. To do this, you need to lead a simple life, free from passions and with less calculation.

—Lao-Tze

November 14 - Purity

"As long as the light is with you, believe in the light, that you may be the sons of light."

—Jesus / John 12:36

Truth is always true, and evil is always evil. Only the madman, doing evil, says that he does it for someone's good. The main and special way to deny the existence of God is to believe as a certainty that public opinion is always unconditionally right and to refuse to attach any importance to God's pervasive influence.

—JOHN RUSKIN

November 15 - Karma

Relatives and friends usually greet a person happily when he is returning home after a long absence. In much the same way, good deeds done here will joyfully greet the departed person, like friends, when he arrives in another world.

—DHAMMAPADA

Do in the day so that at night your sleep is calm, and in youth so that your old age is also calm.

—INDIAN SAYING

November 16 - Objectivity

Only through the eyes of others can you see your flaws.

—CHINESE PROVERB

Each person has a mirror in another in which he can clearly see his own vices, shortcomings and all kinds of his bad sides. However, for the most part, he acts like a dog who barks at the mirror on the assumption that he sees there not himself, but another dog.

—ARTHUR SCHOPENHAUER

November 17 – Non-Existence

Thirty spokes are connected in one empty hub, and the usefulness of the wheel depends on what does not exist, on the emptiness in the hub.

A vessel is made of clay, and its usefulness depends on what doesn't exist, on the emptiness of the vessel.

People make doors and windows in their houses, and from what doesn't exist, from the empty space, the usefulness of the house depends.

Therefore, when things are useful, only that which does not exist in them makes them so.

—Lao-Tze

November 18 – Obstacles

External obstacles do not harm a person with a strong spirit, for harm is all that disfigures and weakens, as happens with animals who find that obstacles anger them. But to the person who meets them with that strength of mind that is given to him, every obstacle adds moral beauty and strength.

—Marcus Aurelius

A man who has never been tempted by happiness or misfortune dies like a soldier who has never encountered an enemy.

—Max Klinger

November 19 – Reverence

A person's happiness depends more on his ability to admire the gifts of others than on his trust in his own. Reverence is the highest gift of man, and all lower animals are happy and noble only because they can share this feeling. The dog honors you, but the fly does not, and this ability to at least partially understand a higher being makes up the nobility of the dog.

—John Ruskin

November 20 – Knowledge

Keep in mind that ignorance never does evil; it is only misconception that does evil. People are mistaken, not because they do not know, but because they imagine themselves to be knowledgeable.

—Jean-Jacques Rousseau

Without leaving the gate or looking out the window, the sage knows what will be by contemplating the heavenly mind. The further you go, the less you may know. Therefore, a holy man, not traveling, has knowledge; not seeing things defines him and, not working, he accomplishes great things.

—Lao-Tze

November 21 – Prayer

"And when you pray, do not be like the hypocrites, for they love to pray standing in the synagogues and on the corners of the streets, in order to appear in front of people. Verily, I say unto you, that they already receive their reward. But when you pray, enter your room and, closing your door, pray to your father, who is unseen, and your father, who sees what is done in secret, will reward you."

—Jesus / Matthew 6:5–6

Acting in keeping with the God-spirit is a form of prayer.

—Talmud

It is best to pray at home, because in a congregation it is impossible to avoid envy, idle talk and slander. Especially during the holidays, when the congregation is going primarily to gossip, it is better not to pray at all.

—Talmud

November 22 – Cleansing

The prayer's deeds preceding the prayer must correspond to the meaning and purpose of his prayer, and if no good deeds preceded the prayer, especially if evil or unkind deeds preceded the prayer, then the one who prays must first repent of his sins and be cleansed of them just as one would put on clean clothes before approaching a gentleman with a request for his help.

Similarly, when a person prays to God through a mouth that is used to speak abominations, slander, unnecessary oaths, etc., this is a gift to God in an unclean case. Therefore, a person must cleanse his tongue and his mouth, and if he sinned with them, then he should try to repent.

—Talmud

November 23 – Desire

Every new desire is the beginning of a new need, the germ of a new sorrow.

—Voltaire

The slave of his passions is the lowest of slaves.

—Yehuda Alharizi

November 24 – Death

When the world began to exist, the mind became its mother. He who knows his mother knows that he is her child, and, knowing this, he is in no danger. When he closes his mouth and closes the gates of his feelings at the end of his life, he will not experience any anxiety.

—Lao-Tze

The dust returns to the ground it came from, and the spirit returns to God who gave it.

—Ecclesiastes 12:7

Bring back his soul as he gave it to you. He gave it to you clean; return it to him clean.

—Talmud

The wise man was asked: "How should one serve invisible spirits?" The sage said: "When we are not yet able to serve people, how can we serve invisible spirits?"

They also asked him: "What is death?" He said: "When

we still don't know what life is, how can we know what death is?"

—CHINESE WISDOM (LE-LUN-YU)

November 25 – Habits

Sow an act, and you will reap a habit; sow a habit and you will reap a character; sow a character, and you will reap your fate.

—WILLIAM MAKEPEACE THACKERAY

There is nothing more important than abstinence if you want to achieve holiness. Abstinence should be an early habit. If it is an early habit, it gains many virtues. For one who has acquired many virtues, there is nothing that he cannot overcome.

—LAO-TZE

Who in his youth was a slave to his passions, that person will in later life be even more in their power. The beginning of evil passion is sweet, but the end is bitter.

—TALMUD

November 26 – Awareness

He who fears the fearless and does not shudder before the truly terrible, he, following a false opinion, enters the path to perdition.

—DHAMMAPADA

He who knows other people is clever, he who knows himself is enlightened.

He who conquers others is powerful, he who conquers himself is even more powerful.

The one who, dying, knows that he is not destroyed, is eternal.

—Lao-Tze

November 27 – Subservience

In full accordance with the grandeur of objects in the line of being is the completeness of their humility to the laws existing for them. The sun and the moon obey the law of universal gravitation in a very clear and obvious manner. However, a particle of dust moves chaotically, but it obeys the same law. The ocean flows and shimmers under the influence not recognized by rivers and lakes.

—John Ruskin

November 28 – Neighbors

"You have heard what is said: 'Love your neighbor and hate your enemy.' But I tell you: love your enemies and pray for those who persecute you so that you may be the children of your Father in heaven. He causes the sun to rise on the evil and the good, and sends rain upon the righteous and the unrighteous."

—Jesus / Matthew 5:43–45

The most perfect of people is the one who loves all his neighbors and does good to them indiscriminately, whether they are good or bad.

—Muhammad

November 29 – Observance

Heaven and earth are great because they have color, image, number, and magnitude. But in man there is something that has neither color, nor image, nor number, nor size —and this is something reasonable.

Consequently, if the world itself were inanimate, then it would be animated by the human mind. But the world is infinite, the human mind is limited, and therefore the human mind cannot be the mind of the whole world.

From this it is clear that the world must be animated by the world mind, and this mind must be infinite.

—Confucius

November 30 – Fruition

Flowers fall off when the fruit begins to grow. Your weaknesses will also disappear when the consciousness of God begins to grow in you.

At least for millennia, darkness filled the space, and it immediately becomes light when light penetrates it. So it is with your soul: no matter how long it has been swallowed by darkness, it will immediately brighten up as soon as God opens his eyes in it.

—Sri Ramakrishna Paramahansa

DECEMBER

December 1 – Elders

If a wise old man tells you to destroy, and a young fool tells you to build, you should destroy, and not create.

When a wise old man says "destroy," he will teach you to create.

When a young fool says "build," he will teach you to destroy.

Show respect to the old man, even if he is too old and incapable of remembering his knowledge.

Even the broken commandments lay in the same ark with the intact tablets.

—Talmud

December 2 – Integrity

It is sad to see people struggle to keep the position they achieved through mere circumstances, rather than living in accord with their intellect and conscience.

A man is told that his actions are good, yet he does not think of them as good, but merely goes on doing what he was doing. Consider the possibility of changing your life for the better.

—Blaise Pascal

December 3 – Duty

One who is close to the law of his duty is on the way to ethics.

One who is close to fulfilling his duty is on the way to virtue.

One who is ashamed that he lacks the power to do his duty is close to achieving this power.

—CHINESE WISDOM

All real truth is achieved by the hard work of self-improvement.

—JOHN RUSKIN

December 4 – Duty

Have you fulfilled your duty? The sole purpose of your short interval of life is to do what He who sent you intended for you to do.

Do you do the right thing?

—LEO TOLSTOY

A man thinks about his way, and God directs his steps.

—TALMUD

December 5 – Judgment

"Do not judge, or you too will be judged. For in the same way you judge others, you will be judged, and with the measure you use, it will be measured to you.

"Why do you look at the speck of sawdust in your brother's eye and pay no attention to the plank in your own eye? How can you say to your brother, 'Let me take the speck out of your eye', when all the time there is a plank in your own eye? You hypocrite, first take the plank out of your own eye, and then you will see clearly to remove the speck from your brother's eye."

—Jesus / Matthew 7:1–5

When you see that someone is in error, do not be angry with him, but try to understand that he does not err through his own will. No one chooses to have a poor understanding. He who errs mistakes the lie for the truth.

But sometimes people reject the truth even when it is revealed to them. These people err willfully, not through misunderstanding, but because the truth reveals their evil actions and eliminates the excuse for their acts. Treat these people not with anger, but with compassion, because their conscience is ill.

—Epictetus

December 6 – Virtue

Our struggles with ourselves result from our own previous sins.

Imagine a mother who tears her child from the mouth of a lion. The child feels pain, but he should connect this pain not to his mother, who is trying to save him, but to the beast who wants to devour him.

One should treat his inner struggle between good and evil in the same way. Like the mother, virtue tries to tear our soul from the jaws of evil. The struggle is painful, but it is necessary and it does us good.

It would have been worse for us if God had left us without this struggle. Virtue cannot appear without it.

—BLAISE PASCAL

December 7 – Progress

To know those who are wise is good.
To abide with them is joy.
Happy are they who do not deal with fools.

—BUDDHIST WISDOM

The wiser and kinder a person is, the more good he can see in other people.

—BLAISE PASCAL

December 8 – Inspiration

I think that the noblest forms of our imagination can guide us in the right direction. These forms have some of the qualities of a dream: inspiration comes suddenly and guides you, and you become like a prophet who does not fully understand his words and actions.

If a person has a good education and upbringing and his

mind is balanced, then his ideas reflect this clearly, as if in a mirror.

But if one's mind is unbalanced, then his ideas reflect it as if in a broken mirror, with all the distortions and mistakes that result from passions and wrong ideas.

—John Ruskin

December 9 – Superficiality

A man does not err until he is enslaved by the spirit of light-heartedness.

—Talmud

The habit of finding humor in everything is a sign of a shallow soul because "funny" things are often shallow.

—Aristotle

Do not think light-heartedly about evil, that it will never touch you. A vessel is filled with water drop by drop. A bad man is filled with evil by doing small bad things, one after another.

Do not think lightly about goodness: that it will never come to you. Consider that a vessel is filled with water, drop after drop. A wise man is filled with goodness by doing small good things, one after another.

—Buddhist wisdom

December 10 – Choice

All is in the power of heaven, except for your choice to serve either God or yourself.

—Talmud

We cannot stop the birds from flying above our heads, but we can stop them from making nests on the top of them. Likewise, we cannot stop bad ideas from appearing in our heads, but we can prevent them from nesting there and hatching into evil deeds.

—Martin Luther

December 11 – Struggle

Self-improvement is difficult, not in itself, but because we have been subject to vices for a long time, and they hinder us on our way.

We cannot blame God for this: if we had no vices, there would be no struggle. The cause of this struggle is our own vices. Yet it is the struggle that will help us: if God were to prevent this struggle, we would have stayed with our vices forever.

—Blaise Pascal

December 12 – Wealth

And he told them this parable: "The ground of a certain rich man yielded an abundant harvest. He thought to himself, 'What shall I do? I have no place to store my crops.'

"Then he said, 'This is what I'll do. I will tear down my barns and build bigger ones, and there I will store my surplus grain.' And I'll say to myself, 'You have plenty of grain laid up for many years. Take life easy: eat, drink and be merry.'

"But God said to him, 'You fool! This very night your life will be demanded from you. Then who will get what you have prepared for yourself?'"

—JESUS / LUKE 12:16–20

"I have my sons, and I have my wealth!" These are the thoughts of a mad man. How can you possess sons and wealth if you do not have possession of yourself?

—BUDDHIST WISDOM

December 13 – Improvement

A wise man was asked, "How can I increase my virtue, get rid of my flaws, and recognize my own intellectual errors?" The wise man answered, "This is a wonderful question: to increase your virtue, you must do your duty without thought of profit; to get rid of your flaws, you must ignore those of others; and to recognize intellectual errors, you must be humble."

—CHINESE WISDOM

December 14 – Time

"Time passes," we are accustomed to say. Yet truly, time stands still, and we are passing.

—TALMUD

Time is behind us, time is before us, and there is no time with us.

—Leo Tolstoy

December 15 - Duality

Every truth has a bit of misconception, and every misconception has a bit of truth in it.

—Heinrich Rickert

The best part of a man only appears alongside his flaws.

—John Ruskin

December 16 - Pleasure

Never look for pleasure purposely, but try to find pleasure in everything. If your hands are busy, then your heart is free and you can find little pleasures in all you hear and see. Do not make the search for pleasure the purpose of your life, for one day your laughter will stop.

—John Ruskin

December 17 - Opinions

Abstain from argument: you cannot truly convince anyone of anything. Opinions are like nails: the more you hammer them, the deeper they go in.

—Juvenal

Experience demonstrates that people have very little control over their tongue, they have less control over it than over anything else.

—Baruch Spinoza

December 18 – Perseverance

What is rooted is easy to nourish. What is recent is easy to correct. What is brittle is easy to break. What is small is easy to scatter.

Consider all things before they appear: a thick tree grows from a tiny shoot; a great tower starts with a few small bricks; a long trip begins with the first step. Be as attentive to the ending as you are to the beginning, and you will complete what you set out to do.

—Lao-Tze

December 19 – Regeneration

"Very truly I tell you, when a kernel of wheat falls to the ground and dies, it seems to remain only a single seed. But in future it will produce many seeds."

—Jesus / John 12:24

The purpose of life lies in filling everything with love. Gradually, slowly but steadily, our life improves as we turn from evil to good, because the good life is the life filled with love.

—Leo Tolstoy

December 20 – Wisdom

A wise nation follows the advice of the wise men, stops fools, and loves all.

—John Ruskin

In the land where wise men govern, they go unnoticed. In the land where fools govern, they are feared or despised.

—Lao-Tze

December 21 – Possessions

You should remember the following great and unchangeable truth: no one but you should possess things that truly and rightfully belong to you.

If you are using your possessions for the development of your life—then they are used properly; otherwise they might become an obstacle to the proper development of your life.

—John Ruskin

December 22 – Charity

Stay simple, kind, clean, god-fearing, just, brave, and forgiving, and do your duties. Try to follow your intellect and your conscience, and maintain the virtue of your brothers.

Life is short. Do not neglect the most important thing: charity.

—Marcus Aurelius

December 23 – Insults

My children! If someone should abuse you with his tongue, do not pay too much attention to this: it is a small thing. Meet with him and make peace with him, or ask for your friends' help, and make it a complete peace.

—Talmud

December 24 – Effort

The path to real knowledge is not always over soft grass. Often you must climb bare rocks on your way.

—John Ruskin

Bad deeds are easy. Good deeds require considerable effort.

—Dhammapada

December 25 – Miscellany

Control yourself to the extent that you respect others as much you respect yourself and treat them as you would like to be treated. This is the act of loving people. There is nothing superior to this.

—Confucius

People try a thousand times harder to improve their wealth than to improve their intellect and heart; yet for our own happiness, what is inside a person is much more important than what he possesses.

—Arthur Schopenhauer

December 26 – Humility

"No one who puts a hand to the plow and looks back is fit for service in the kingdom of God."

—Jesus / Luke 9:62

True virtue does not look back at its shadow, which is worldly fame.

—Johann Wolfgang von Goethe

December 27 – Self-Improvement

"The root of evil is not to know the truth," the Buddha said. "The tree of suffering grows from this root, and bears many fruits. There is only one way to fight ignorance: through knowledge. This can be achieved only by your own work of self-improvement."

Our attempts to improve the life of others are in vain. The best way to improve the well-being of the whole world is to improve the well-being of a single person, and you should start with yourself.

—Frank Hartman

December 28 – Piety

Even the smallest and the least important deed may serve a great purpose. This is especially important if we want to serve God.

—Leo Tolstoy

December 29 - Miscellany

When you understand that all that is created can be destroyed, you will find the things that are eternal.

—Buddhist wisdom

God can see everything, yet God is invisible. Likewise, our soul cannot be seen, but it can see.

—Talmud

A person lives by intellect. Do not attribute life to a body. Your body is just a vessel that includes this inner force. The outer shell lives only by the inner force of intellect; without this, it is like a pen without an author.

—Marcus Aurelius

December 30 - Transgressions

If you break a small commandment, you will soon break a big one. If you break the commandment "love the other just as yourself" then you will break other things that are not allowed: you will hate your brother, and then finally you will shed another's blood.

—Talmud

December 31 - Knowledge

Every developed mind rejoices with the amount of knowledge it has about this world; yet it rejoices even more by understanding that there is a much greater amount of knowledge that we do not yet possess.

—John Ruskin

Knowledge is limitless: he who is the most educated among the wise men is as far from true knowledge as the most ignorant man.

—John Ruskin

Knowledge of the laws of life is much more important than any other knowledge; and the knowledge that leads to self-improvement is the most important knowledge of all.

—Herbert Spencer

Tolstoy's Note on His Translations of the Aphorisms

I TOOK THE THOUGHTS collected here from a very large number of works and collections. I indicated the author of each thought beneath it, though I did not mark the exact source or book title or work from which I took it. In some cases, I translated these thoughts not directly from their original sources, but from a translation from the languages in which they became known to me, so sometimes my translations might not be completely identical to the originals.

When I translated thoughts by German, French or Italian thinkers, I did not strictly follow the original, usually making it shorter and easier to understand, and omitting some words. Readers might tell me that a quote is not then Pascal or Rousseau but my own work. Yet I think that there is nothing wrong in conveying their thoughts in a modified form.

Therefore, if someone wants to translate this book into

other languages, I would like to advise them not to look for the original quotes from the English poet Coleridge, say, or the German philosopher Kant, or the French writer Rousseau, but to translate directly from my writing.

Another reason some of these thoughts may not correspond to the originals is at times I took a thought from a lengthy and convoluted argument, and I had to change some words and phrases for clarity and unity of expression. In some cases, I even express the thought entirely in my own words.

I did this because the purpose of my book is not to give exact, word-for-word translations of thoughts created by other authors. It is to use the great and fruitful intellectual heritage created by different writers to present for a wide-reading audience an easily accessible, everyday circle of reading which will arouse their best thoughts and feelings.

I hope that the readers of this book may experience the same benevolent and elevating feeling which I have experienced when I was working on its creation, and which I experience again and again, when I reread it every day.

March 1908

What Men Live By

I

A SHOEMAKER LIVED in a peasant's hut with his wife and children. He had neither a proper house nor land of his own. Bread was dear, his prices were low. Nearly all that he earned from his cobbling was spent on their food.

The shoemaker and his wife had only one sheepskin coat between them and it was old and torn to tatters. It was the second year he had been wanting to buy sheepskins for a new coat. By autumn this shoemaker had saved a little money: a three-rouble paper note was hidden in his wife's box. He was also owed five roubles and twenty kopeks by farmers in the village.

On a cold morning he prepared himself to go to the village to buy the sheepskins. Over his shirt he put on his wife's wadded jacket, the one she had made for herself, and he also put on his thin cloth coat. He cut himself a stick to serve as a staff, and started off after breakfast with their three-rouble note in his pocket.

He thought to himself: "I'll collect the five roubles that are due to me and add the three I have got, and that will be enough to buy sheepskins for the winter coat."

He came to the village and called at a peasant's hut who owed him money, but the man was not at home. The peasant's wife promised that the money should be paid next week, but she could not pay it herself. Then the shoemaker called on another peasant who owed him money, but this one also swore he had no money, and would only pay twenty kopeks which he owed for a pair of boots the shoemaker had mended. The shoemaker then tried to buy the sheepskins on credit, but the dealer would not trust him.

"Bring your money," said he, "then you may have your pick of the skins. We know what debt-collecting is like."

So, all the business the shoemaker did was to get the twenty kopeks for boots he had mended, and to take a pair of felt boots a peasant gave him to sole with leather.

The shoemaker felt downhearted. He spent the twenty kopeks on vodka, and started homewards without having bought any skins. In the morning he had felt the frost but now, after drinking the vodka, he felt warm, even without a sheepskin coat. He trudged along, striking his stick on the frozen earth with one hand, swinging the felt boots with the other, and talking to himself.

"I'm quite warm," said he, "though I have no sheepskin coat. I've had a drop, and it runs through all my veins. I need no sheepskins. I go along and don't worry about anything. That's the sort of man I am! What do I care? I can live without sheepskins. I don't need them. My wife will fret, to be sure. And, true enough, it is a shame; one works all day long, and then does not get paid. Stop a bit! If you don't bring that money along, sure enough I'll skin you, blessed if I don't. How's that? He pays twenty kopeks at a time! What can I do with twenty kopeks? Drink it—that's all one can do! Hard up, he says he is! So, he may be—but what about me? You have house and cattle, and everything; I've only what I stand up in! You have corn of your own growing; I have to buy every grain. Do what I will, I must spend three roubles every week for bread alone. I come home and find the bread all used up, and I have to fork out another rouble and a half. So just pay up what you owe, and no nonsense about it!"

By this time he had nearly reached the shrine at the bend of the road. Looking up, he saw something whitish behind the shrine. The daylight was fading, and the shoemaker peered at the thing without being able to make out what it was. "There was no white stone here before. Can it be an ox? It's not like an ox. It has a head like a man, but it's too white; and what could a man be doing there?"

He came closer, so that it was clearly visible. To his surprise it really was a man, alive or dead, sitting naked, leaning motionless against the shrine. Terror seized the shoemaker, and he thought, "Someone has killed him, stripped him, and left him here. If I meddle I shall surely get into trouble."

So, the shoemaker went on. He passed in front of the shrine so that he could not see the man. When he had gone some way, he looked back, and saw that the man was no longer leaning against the shrine, but was moving and seemed to be looking towards him. The shoemaker felt more frightened than before, and thought, "Shall I go back to him, or shall I go on? If I go near him something dreadful may happen. Who knows who the fellow is? He has not come here for any good. If I go near him he may jump up and throttle me, and there will be no getting away. Or if not, he'd still be a burden on one's hands. What could I do with a naked man? I couldn't give him my last clothes. Heaven only help me to get away!"

So, the shoemaker hurried on, leaving the shrine behind him—when suddenly his conscience smote him, and he stopped in the road.

"What are you doing, Simon?" said he to himself. "The man may be dying of want, and you slip past afraid. Have you grown so rich as to be afraid of robbers? Ah, Simon, shame on you!"

So, he turned back.

II

SIMON APPROACHED THE stranger, looked at him, and saw that he was a young man, fit, with no bruises on his body, only evidently freezing and frightened, and he sat there leaning back without looking up at Simon, as if too faint to look up. Simon went up to him, and then the man seemed to wake up. Turning his head, he opened his eyes and looked into Simon's face. That one look was enough to make Simon fond of the man. He threw the felt boots on the ground, undid his sash, laid it on the boots, and took off his cloth coat.

"It's not a time for talking," said he. "Come, put this coat on at once!" And Simon took the man by the elbows and helped him to rise. As he stood there, Simon saw that his body was clean and in good condition, his hands and feet shapely, and his face good and kind. He threw his coat over the man's shoulders, but the latter could not find the sleeves. Simon guided his arms into them, and drawing the coat well on, wrapped it closely about him, tying the sash round the man's waist.

Simon even took off his torn cap to put it on the man's head, but then his own head felt cold, and he thought: "I'm quite bald, while he has long curly hair." So he put his cap on his own head again. "It will be better to give him something for his feet," thought he; and he made the man sit down, and helped him to put on the felt boots, saying, "There, friend, now move about and warm yourself. Other matters can be settled later on. Can you walk?"

The man stood up and looked kindly at Simon, but did not say a word.

"Why don't you speak?" said Simon. "It's too cold to stay here; we must be getting home. There now, take my stick, and if you're feeling weak, lean on that. Now step out!"

The man started walking, and moved easily, not lagging behind.

As they went along, Simon asked him, "And where do you belong to?"

"I'm not from these parts."

"I thought as much. I know the folks hereabouts. But, how did you come to be there by the shrine?"

"I cannot tell."

"Has someone been ill-treating you?"

"No one has ill-treated me. God has punished me."

"Of course, God rules all. Still, you'll have to find food and shelter somewhere. Where do you want to go to?"

"It is all the same to me."

Simon was amazed. The man did not look like a rogue, and he spoke gently, yet he gave no account of himself.

Still Simon thought, "Who knows what may have happened?' And he said to the stranger: 'Well then, come home with me, and at least warm yourself awhile."

So, Simon walked towards his home, and the stranger kept up with him, walking at his side. The wind had risen and Simon felt it cold under his shirt. He was getting over his tipsiness by now, and began to feel the frost. He went along sniffling and wrapping his wife's jacket round him, and he thought to himself: "There now—talk about sheepskins! I went out for sheepskins and come home without even a coat to my back, and what is more, I'm bringing a naked man along with me. Matrena won't be pleased!" And when he thought of his wife, he felt sad; but when he looked at the stranger and remembered how he had looked up at him at the shrine, his heart was glad.

III

SIMON'S WIFE HAD everything ready early that day. She had cut wood, brought water, fed the children, eaten her own meal, and now she sat thinking. She wondered when she ought to make bread: now or tomorrow? There was still a large piece left.

"If Simon has had some dinner in town," thought she, "and does not eat much for supper, the bread will last out another day."

She weighed the piece of bread in her hand again and again, and thought: "I won't make any more today. We have only enough flour left to bake one batch. We can manage to make this last out till Friday."

So Matrena put away the bread, and sat down at the table to patch her husband's shirt. While she worked, she thought how her husband was buying skins for a warm winter coat.

"If only the dealer does not cheat him. My good man is much too simple; he cheats nobody, but any child can take him in. Eight roubles is a lot of money—he should get a good coat at that price. Not tanned skins, but still a proper winter coat. How difficult it was last winter to get on without a warm coat. I could neither get down to the river, nor go out anywhere. When he went out, he put on all we had, and there was nothing left for me. He did not start very early today, but still it's time he was back. I only hope he has not gone on the spree!"

Hardly had Matrena thought this, when steps were heard on the threshold, and someone entered. Matrena stuck her needle into her work and went out into the passage. There she saw two men: Simon, and with him a man without a hat, and wearing felt boots.

Matrena noticed at once that her husband smelt of spirits. "There now, he has been drinking," thought she. And when she saw that he was coatless, had only her jacket on, brought no parcel, stood there silent, and seemed ashamed, her heart was ready to break with disappointment. "He has drunk the money," thought she, "and has been on the spree with some good-for-nothing fellow whom he has brought home with him."

Matrena let them pass into the hut, followed them in, and saw that the stranger was a young, slight man, who was wearing her husband's coat. There was no shirt to be seen under it, and he had no hat. Having entered, he stood neither moving, nor raising his eyes, and Matrena thought: "He must be a bad man—he's afraid."

Matrena frowned, and stood beside the oven looking to see what they would do.

Simon took off his cap and sat down on the bench as if things were all right.

"Come, Matrena; if supper is ready, let us have some."

Matrena muttered something to herself and did not move, but stayed where she was, by the oven. She looked first at the one and then at the other of them, and only shook her head. Simon saw that his wife was annoyed, but tried to pass it off. Pretending not to notice anything, he took the stranger by the arm.

"Sit down, friend," said he, "and let us have some supper."

The stranger sat down on the bench.

"Haven't you cooked anything for us?" said Simon.

Matrena's anger boiled over. "I've cooked, but not for you. It seems to me you have drunk your wits away. You went to buy a sheepskin coat, but come home without so much as the coat you had on, and bring a naked vagabond home with you. I have no supper for drunkards like you."

"That's enough, Matrena. Don't wag your tongue without reason. You had better ask what sort of man—"

"And you tell me what you've done with the money?"

Simon found the pocket of the jacket, drew out the three-rouble note, and unfolded it.

"Here is the money. Trífonof did not pay, but promises to pay soon."

Matrena became still more angry; he had bought no sheepskins, but had put his only coat on some naked fellow and had even brought him to their house.

She snatched up the note from the table, took it to put away in safety, and said: "I have no supper for you. We can't feed all the naked drunkards in the world."

"There now, Matrena, hold your tongue a bit. First hear what a man has to say—"

"Much wisdom I shall hear from a drunken fool. I was right in not wanting to marry you, a drunkard. The linen my mother gave me you drank; and now you've been to buy a coat, and have drunk the money for that, too!"

Simon tried to explain to his wife that he had only spent twenty kopeks; tried to tell how he had found the man—but Matrena would not let him get a word in. She began talking without stopping, and dragged in things that had happened ten years before.

Matrena talked and talked, and at last she flew at Simon and seized him by the sleeve.

"Give me my jacket. It is the only one I have, and you must needs take it from me and wear it yourself. Give it here, you mangy dog, and may the devil take you."

Simon began to pull off the jacket, and turned a sleeve of it inside out; Matrena seized the jacket and it burst its seams. She snatched it up, threw it over her head and went to the door. She meant to go out, but stopped undecided—she wanted to work off her anger, but she also wanted to learn what sort of a man the stranger was.

IV

MATRENA STOPPED and said: "If he were a good man he would not be naked. Why, he hasn't even a shirt on him. If he were all right, you would say where you came across the fellow."

"That's just what I am trying to tell you," said Simon. "As I came to the shrine I saw him sitting all naked and frozen. It isn't quite the weather to sit about naked! God sent me to him, or he would have perished. What was I to do? How do we know what may have happened to him? So I took him, clothed him, and brought him along. Don't be so angry, Matrena. It is a sin. Remember, we all must die one day."

Angry words rose to Matrena's lips, but she looked at the stranger and was silent. He sat on the edge of the bench, motionless, his hands folded on his knees, his head drooping on his breast, his eyes closed, and his brows knit as if in pain. Matrena was silent, and Simon said: "Matrena, have you no love of God?"

Matrena heard these words, and as she looked at the stranger, suddenly her heart softened towards him. She came back from the door, and going to the oven she got out the supper. Setting a cup on the table, she poured out some broth. Then she brought out the last piece of bread, and set out a knife and spoons.

"Eat, if you want to," said she.

Simon drew the stranger to the table.

"Take your place, young man," said he.

Simon cut the bread, crumbled it into the broth, and they began to eat. Matrena sat at the corner of the table, resting her head on her hand and looking at the stranger.

And Matrena was touched with pity for the stranger, and began to feel fond of him. And at once the stranger's face lit up; his brows were no longer bent, he raised his eyes and smiled at Matrena.

When they had finished supper, the woman cleared

away the things and began questioning the stranger. "Where are you from?"

"I am not from these parts."

"But how did you come to be on the road?"

"I may not tell."

"Did someone rob you?"

"God punished me."

"And you were lying there naked?"

"Yes, naked and freezing. Simon saw me and had pity on me. He took off his coat, put it on me and brought me here. And you have fed me, given me drink, and shown pity on me. God will reward you!"

Matrena rose, took from the window Simon's old shirt she had been patching, and gave it to the stranger. She also brought out a pair of trousers for him.

"There," said she, "I see you have no shirt. Put this on, and lie down where you please, in the loft or on the oven."

The stranger took off the coat, put on the shirt, and went up to lie down in the loft. Matrena put out the candle, took the coat, and climbed to where her husband lay.

Matrena drew the skirts of the coat over her and lay down, but could not sleep; she could not get the stranger out of her mind.

When she remembered that he had eaten their last piece of bread and that there was none for tomorrow, and thought of the shirt and trousers she had given away, she felt sad, but when she remembered how he had smiled, her heart was glad.

Long did Matrena lie awake, and she noticed that Simon also was awake—he drew the coat towards him.

"Simon!"

"Well?"

"You have had the last of the bread, and I have not put any to rise. I don't know what we shall do tomorrow. Perhaps I can borrow some of neighbor Martha."

"If we're alive we shall find something to eat."

The woman lay still awhile, and then said, "He seems a good man, but why does he not tell us who he is?"

"I suppose he has his reasons."

"Simon!"

"Well?"

"We give but why does nobody give us anything?"

Simon did not know what to say; so he only said, "Let us stop talking," and turned over and went to sleep.

V

IN THE MORNING SIMON awoke and went downstairs. The children were still asleep; his wife had gone to the neighbor's to borrow some bread. The stranger was sitting on the bench, dressed in the old shirt and trousers, and looking up and around. His face was brighter than it had been the day before.

Simon said to him, "Well, friend the belly wants bread, and the naked body clothes. One has to work for a living. What work do you know?"

"I do not know any."

This surprised Simon, but he said, "Men who want to learn can learn anything."

"Men work, and I will work also."

"What is your name?"

"Michael."

"Well, Michael, if you don't wish to talk about yourself, that is your own affair but you'll have to earn a living for yourself. If you will work as I tell you, I will give you food and shelter."

"May God reward you! I will learn. Show me what to do."

Simon took yarn, put it round his thumb and began to twist it.

"It is easy enough—see!"

Michael watched him, put some yarn round his own thumb in the same way, caught the knack, and twisted the yarn also.

Then Simon showed him how to wax the thread. This also Michael mastered. Next Simon showed him how to twist the bristle in, and how to sew, and this, too, Michael learned at once.

Whatever Simon showed him he understood at once, and after three days he worked as if he had sewn boots all his life. He worked without stopping and ate little. When work was over he sat silently, looking upwards. He hardly went into the street, spoke only when necessary, and neither joked nor laughed. They never saw him smile, except that first evening when Matrena gave them supper.

VI

DAY BY DAY AND WEEK by week the year went round. Michael lived and worked with Simon. His fame spread till people said that no one had ever sewed boots so neatly and so strongly as Simon's workman, Michael; and from all the district round people came to Simon for their boots, and he began to be well off.

One winter day, as Simon and Michael sat working, a carriage on sledge-runners, with three horses and with bells, drove up to the hut. They looked out of the window; the carriage stopped at their door, a fine servant jumped down from the box and opened the door. A gentleman in a fur coat got out and walked up to Simon's hut. Up jumped Matrena and opened the door wide. The gentleman stooped to enter the hut, and when he drew himself up again his head nearly reached the ceiling. He seemed quite to fill his end of the room.

Simon rose, bowed, and looked at the gentleman with astonishment. He had never seen anyone like him. Simon himself was lean, Michael was thin, and Matrena was dry as a bone, but this man was like someone from another world: red-faced, burly, with a neck like a bull's, and looking altogether as if he were cast in iron.

The gentleman puffed, threw off his fur coat, sat down on the bench, and said, "Which of you is the master bootmaker?"

"I am, your Excellency," said Simon, coming forward.

Then the gentleman shouted to his lad, "Hey, Fédka, bring the leather!"

The servant ran in, bringing a parcel. The gentleman took the parcel and put it on the table.

"Untie it," said he. The lad untied it.

The gentleman pointed to the leather.

"Look, shoemaker," said he, "do you see this leather?"

"Yes, your honor."

"But do you know what sort of leather it is?"

Simon felt the leather and said, "It is good leather."

"Good, indeed! Why, you fool, you never saw such leather before in your life. It's German, and cost twenty roubles."

Simon was frightened, and said, "Where should I ever see leather like that?"

"Just so! Now, can you make it into boots for me?"

"Yes, your Excellency, I can."

Then the gentleman shouted at him: "You can, can you? Well, remember whom you are to make them for, and what the leather is. You must make me boots that will wear for a year, neither losing shape nor coming unsewn. If you can do it, take the leather and cut it up, but if you can't, say so. I warn you now if your boots become unsewn or lose shape within a year, I will have you put in prison. If they don't burst or lose shape for a year I will pay you ten roubles for your work."

Simon was frightened, and did not know what to say. He glanced at Michael and, nudging him with his elbow, whispered: "Shall I take the work?"

Michael nodded his head as if to say, "Yes, take it."

Simon did as Michael advised, and undertook to make boots that would not lose shape or split for a whole year.

Calling his servant, the gentleman told him to pull the boot off his left leg, which he stretched out.

"Take my measure!" said he.

Simon stitched a paper measure seventeen inches long, smoothed it out, knelt down, wiped his hands well on his apron so as not to soil the gentleman's sock, and began to measure. He measured the sole, and round the instep, and began to measure the calf of the leg, but the paper was too short. The calf of the leg was as thick as a beam.

"Mind you don't make it too tight in the leg."

Simon stitched on another strip of paper. The gentleman twitched his toes about in his sock, looking round at those in the hut, and as he did so he noticed Michael.

"Who have you there?" asked he.

"That is my workman. He will sew the boots."

"Mind," said the gentleman to Michael, "remember to make them so that they will last me a year."

Simon also looked at Michael, and saw that Michael was not looking at the gentleman, but was gazing into the corner behind the gentleman, as if he saw someone there. Michael looked and looked, and suddenly he smiled, and his face became brighter.

"What are you grinning at, you fool?" thundered the gentleman. "You had better look to it that the boots are ready in time."

"They shall be ready in good time," said Michael.

"Mind it is so," said the gentleman, and he put on his boots and his fur coat, wrapped the coat round him, and went to the door. But he forgot to stoop, and struck his head against the lintel.

He swore and rubbed his head. Then he took his seat in the carriage and drove away.

When he had gone, Simon said: "There's a figure of a man for you! You could not kill him with a mallet. He almost knocked out the lintel, but little harm it did him."

And Matrena said: "Living as he does, how should he not grow strong? Death itself can't touch such a rock as that."

VII

THEN SIMON SAID TO Michael: "Well, we have taken the work, but we must see we don't get into trouble over it. The leather is dear, and the gentleman hot-tempered.

We must make no mistakes. Come, your eye is truer and your hands have become nimbler than mine, so you take this measure and cut out the boots. I will finish off the sewing of the vamps."

Michael did as he was told. He took the leather, spread it out on the table, folded it in two, took a knife and began to cut out.

Matrena came and watched him cutting, and was surprised to see how he was doing it. Matrena was accustomed to seeing boots made, and she looked and saw that Michael was not cutting the leather for boots, but was cutting it round.

She wished to say something, but she thought to herself: "Perhaps I do not understand how gentlemen's boots should be made. I suppose Michael knows more about it—and I won't interfere."

When Michael had cut up the leather, he took a thread and began to sew not with two ends, as boots are sewn, but with a single end, as for soft slippers.

Again, Matrena wondered, but again she did not interfere. Michael sewed on steadily till noon. Then Simon rose for dinner, looked around, and saw that Michael had made slippers out of the gentleman's leather.

"Ah," groaned Simon, and he thought, "How is it that Michael, who has been with me a whole year and never made a mistake before, should do such a dreadful thing? The gentleman ordered high boots, welted, with whole fronts, and Michael has made soft slippers with single soles, and has wasted the leather. What am I to say to the gentleman? I can never replace leather such as this."

And he said to Michael, "What are you doing, friend?

You have ruined me! You know the gentleman ordered high boots, but see what you have made!"

Hardly had he begun to rebuke Michael, when *rat-tat* went the iron ring that hung at the door. Someone was knocking. They looked out of the window; a man had come on horseback, and was fastening his horse. They opened the door, and the servant who had been with the gentleman came in.

"Good day," said he.

"Good day," replied Simon. "What can we do for you?"

"My mistress has sent me about the boots."

"What about the boots?"

"Why, my master no longer needs them. He is dead."

"Is it possible?"

"He did not live to get home after leaving you but died in the carriage. When we reached home and the servants came to help him alight, he rolled over like a sack. He was dead already, and so stiff that he could hardly be got out of the carriage. My mistress sent me here, saying: 'Tell the bootmaker that the gentleman who ordered boots of him and left the leather for them no longer needs the boots, but that he must quickly make soft slippers for the corpse. Wait till they are ready, and bring them back with you.' That is why I have come."

Michael reached down and gathered up the remnants of the leather, rolled them up, took the soft slippers he had made, slapped them together, wiped them down with his apron, and handed them all to the servant, who took them and said: "Goodbye, masters, and good day to you!"

VIII

ANOTHER YEAR PASSED, and another, and Michael was now living his sixth year with Simon. He lived as before. He went nowhere, only spoke when necessary, and had only smiled twice in all those years—once when Matrena gave him food, and a second time when the gentleman was in their hut. Simon was more than pleased with his workman. He never now asked him where he came from, and only feared lest Michael should go away.

They were all at home one day. Matrena was putting iron pots in the oven; the children were running along the benches and looking out of the window; Simon was sewing at one window, and Michael was fastening on a heel at the other.

One of the boys ran along the bench to Michael, leant on his shoulder, and looked out of the window.

"Look, Uncle Michael! There is a lady with little girls! She seems to be coming here. And one of the girls is lame."

When the boy said that, Michael dropped his work, turned to the window, and looked out into the street.

Simon was surprised. Michael never used to look out into the street, but now he pressed against the window, staring at something. Simon also looked out, and saw that a well-dressed woman was really coming to his hut, leading by the hand two little girls in fur coats and warm woolen shawls. The girls could hardly be told one from the other, except that one of them was crippled in her left leg and walked with a limp.

The woman stepped into the porch and entered the passage. Feeling about for the entrance she found the latch, which she lifted, and opened the door. She let the two girls go in first, and followed them into the hut.

"Good day, good folk!"

"Pray come in," said Simon. "What can we do for you?" The woman sat down by the table. The two little girls pressed close to her knees, afraid of the people in the hut.

"I want leather shoes made for these two little girls, for spring."

"We can do that. We have never made such small shoes, but we can make them—either welted or turnover shoes, linen lined. My man, Michael, is a master at the work."

Simon glanced at Michael and saw that he had left his work and was sitting with his eyes fixed on the little girls. Simon was surprised. It was true the girls were pretty. They had black eyes, were plump, and rosy-cheeked, and they wore nice warm shawls and fur coats, but still Simon could not understand why Michael should look at them like that—just as if he had known them before.

He was puzzled, but went on talking with the woman, and arranging the price. Having fixed it, he prepared the measure. The woman lifted the lame girl on to her lap and said: "Take two measures from this little girl. Make one shoe for the lame foot and three for the sound one. They both have the same-sized feet. They are twins."

Simon took the measure and, speaking of the lame girl, said: "How did it happen to her? She is such a pretty girl. Was she born so?"

"No, her mother crushed her leg."

Then Matrena joined in. She wondered who this woman was, and whose the children were, so she asked: "Are not you their mother then?"

"No, my good woman; I am neither their mother nor any relation to them. They were quite strangers to me, but I adopted them."

"They are not your children and yet you are so fond of them?"

"How can I help being fond of them? I fed them both at my own breasts. I had a child of my own, but God took him. I was not so fond of him as I now am of them."

"Then whose children are they?"

IX

THE WOMAN, having begun talking, told them the whole story.

"It is about six years since their parents died, both in one week: their father was buried on the Tuesday, and their mother died on the Friday. These orphans were born three days after their father's death, and their mother did not live another day. My husband and I were then living as peasants in the village. We were neighbors of theirs, our yard being next to theirs.

"Their father was a lonely man, a wood-cutter in the forest. When the men were falling trees one day, they let one fall on him. It fell across his body and crushed his bowels out. They hardly got him home before his soul went to God; and that same week his wife gave birth to twins—these little girls. She was poor and alone; she had no one, young or old, with her. Alone she gave them birth, and alone she met her death.

"The next morning I went to see her, but when I entered the hut, she, poor thing, was already stark and cold. In dying she had rolled on to this child and crushed her leg. The village folk came to the hut, washed the body, laid her out, made a coffin, and buried her. They were good folk. The babies were left alone. What was to be done with them? I was the only woman there who had a baby at the time. I was nursing my first-born—eight weeks old. So I took them for a time.

"The peasants came together, and thought and thought what to do with them; and at last they said to me: 'For the present, Mary, you had better keep the girls, and later on we will arrange what to do for them.' So I nursed the sound one at my breast, but at first I did not feed this crippled one. I did not suppose she would live.

"Then I thought to myself, why should the poor innocent suffer? I pitied her, and began to feed her. And so I fed my own boy and these two—the three of them—at my own breast. I was young and strong, and had good food, and God gave me so much milk that at times it even overflowed.

"I used sometimes to feed two at a time, while the third was waiting. When one had enough I nursed the third. And God so ordered it that these grew up, while my own was buried before he was two years old. And I had no more children, though we prospered. Now my husband is working for the corn merchant at the mill. The pay is good, and we are well off. But I have no children of my own, and how lonely I should be without these little girls! How can I help loving them! They are the joy of my life!"

She pressed the lame little girl to her with one hand, while with the other she wiped the tears from her cheeks.

And Matrena sighed, and said: "The proverb is true that says, 'One may live without father or mother, but one cannot live without God.'"

So they talked together, when suddenly the whole hut was lit up as though by summer lightning from the corner where Michael sat. They all looked towards him and saw him sitting, his hands folded on his knees, gazing upwards and smiling.

X

THE WOMAN WENT away with the girls. Michael rose from the bench, put down his work, and took off his apron. Then, bowing low to Simon and his wife, he said: "Farewell, masters. God has forgiven me. I ask your forgiveness, too, for anything done amiss."

And they saw that a light shone from Michael. And Simon rose, bowed down to Michael, and said: "I see, Michael, that you are no common man, and I can neither keep you nor question you. Only tell me this: how is it that when I found you and brought you home, you were gloomy, and when my wife gave you food you smiled at her and became brighter? Then when the gentleman came to order the boots, you smiled again and became brighter still? And now, when this woman brought the little girls, you smiled a third time, and have become as bright as day? Tell me, Michael, why does your face shine so, and why did you smile those three times?"

And Michael answered: "Light shines from me because I have been punished, but now God has pardoned me. And I smiled three times, because God sent me to learn three truths, and I have learnt them. One I learnt when your wife pitied me, and that is why I smiled the first time. The second I learnt when the rich man ordered the boots, and then I smiled again. And now, when I saw those little girls, I learnt the third and last truth, and I smiled the third time."

And Simon said, "Tell me, Michael, what did God punish you for? And what were the three truths? that I, too, may know them."

And Michael answered: "God punished me for disobeying Him. I was an angel in heaven and disobeyed God. God sent me to fetch a woman's soul. I flew to earth, and saw a sick woman lying alone, who had just given birth to twin girls. They moved feebly at their mother's side, but she could not lift them to her breast. When she saw me, she understood that God had sent me for her soul, and she wept and said: 'Angel of God! My husband has just been buried, killed by a falling tree. I have neither sister, nor aunt, nor mother: no one to care for my orphans. Do not take my soul! Let me nurse my babes, feed them, and set them on their feet before I die. Children cannot live without father or mother.'

"And I hearkened to her. I placed one child at her breast and gave the other into her arms, and returned to the Lord in heaven. I flew to the Lord, and said: 'I could not take the soul of the mother. Her husband was killed by a tree; the woman has twins, and prays that her soul may not be taken.' She says: 'Let me nurse and feed my children, and set them on their feet. Children cannot live without father or mother.' I have not taken her soul."

And God said: "Go—take the mother's soul, and learn three truths: Learn What dwells in man, What is not given to man, and What men live by. When thou hast learnt these things, thou shalt return to heaven."

"So I flew again to earth and took the mother's soul. The babes dropped from her breasts. Her body rolled over on the bed and crushed one babe, twisting its leg. I rose above the village, wishing to take her soul to God; but a wind seized me, and my wings drooped and dropped off. Her soul rose alone to God, while I fell to earth by the roadside."

XI

AND SIMON AND MATRENA understood who it was that had lived with them, and whom they had clothed and fed. And they wept with awe and with joy. And the angel said: "I was alone in the field, naked. I had never known human needs—cold and hunger—till I became a man. I was famished, frozen, and did not know what to do. I saw, near the field I was in, a shrine built for God, and I went to it hoping to find shelter. But the shrine was locked, and I could not enter. So I sat down behind the shrine to shelter myself at least from the wind.

"Evening drew on. I was hungry, frozen, and in pain. Suddenly I heard a man coming along the road. He carried a pair of felt boots, and was talking to himself. For the first time since I became a man I saw the mortal face of a man, and his face seemed terrible to me and I turned from it. And I heard the man talking to himself of how to cover his body from the cold in winter, and how to feed his wife and children."

And I thought: "I am perishing of cold and hunger, and here is a man thinking only of how to clothe himself and his wife, and how to get bread for themselves. He cannot help me.

"When the man saw me he frowned and became still more terrible, and he passed me by on the other side.

I despaired, but suddenly I heard him coming back. I looked up, and did not recognize the same man: before, I had seen death in his face; but now he was alive, and I recognized in him the presence of God.

"He came up to me, clothed me, took me with him, and brought me to his home. When I entered the house, a woman came to meet us and began to speak. The woman was still more terrible than the man had been; the spirit of death came from her mouth. I could not breathe for the stench of death that spread around her.

"She wished to drive me out into the cold, and I knew that if she did so she would die. Suddenly her husband spoke to her of God, and the woman changed at once. And when she brought me food and looked at me, I glanced at her and saw that death no longer dwelt in her; she had become alive, and in her too I saw God.

"Then I remembered the first lesson God had set me: 'Learn what dwells in man.' And I understood that in man dwells Love! I was glad that God had already begun to show me what He had promised, and I smiled for the first time. But I had not yet learnt all. I did not yet know What is not given to man, and What men live by.

"I lived with you, and a year passed. A man came to order boots that should wear for a year without losing shape or cracking. I looked at him, and suddenly, behind his shoulder, I saw my comrade—the angel of death. None but me saw that angel, but I knew him, and knew that before the sun set he would take that rich man's soul. And I thought to myself, 'The man is making preparations for a year, and does not know that he will die before evening.' And I remembered God's second saying, 'Learn what is not given to man.'

"What dwells in man I already knew. Now I learnt what is not given him. It is not given to man to know his own needs. And I smiled for the second time. I was glad to have seen my comrade angel—glad also that God had revealed to me the meaning of the second saying.

"But I still did not know all. I did not know What men live by. And I lived on, waiting till God should reveal to me the last lesson. In the sixth year came the girl-twins with the woman; and I recognized the girls, and heard how they had been kept alive. Having heard the story, I thought, 'Their mother besought me for the children's sake, and I believed her when she said that children cannot live without father or mother, but a stranger has nursed them, and has brought them up.' And when the woman showed her love for the children that were not her own, and wept over them, I saw in her the living God and understood What men live by. And I knew that God had revealed to me the last lesson, and had forgiven my sin. And then I smiled for the third time."

XII

AND THE ANGEL'S BODY became bare, and he was clothed in light so that the eye could not look on him; and his voice grew louder, as though it came not from him but from heaven above. And the angel said:

"I have learnt that all men live not by care for themselves but by love.

"It was not given to the mother to know what her children needed for their life. Nor was it given to the rich man to know what he himself needed. Nor is it given to any man to know whether, when evening comes, he will need boots for his body or slippers for his corpse.

"I remained alive when I was a man, not by care of myself, but because love was present in a passerby, and because he and his wife pitied and loved me. The orphans remained alive, not because of their mother's care, but because there was love in the heart of a woman who was a stranger to them, who pitied and loved them. And all men live not by what they spend on their own welfare, but because love exists in man.

"I knew before that God gave life to men and desires that they should live; now I understood more than that.

"I understood that God does not wish men to live apart, and therefore he does not reveal to them what each one needs for himself. But he wishes them to live united, and therefore reveals to each of them what is necessary for all.

"I have now understood that though it seems to men that they live to care for themselves, in truth it is love alone by which they live. He who has love is in God, and God is in him, for God is love."

And the angel sang praise to God, so that the hut trembled at his voice. The roof opened, and a column of fire rose from earth to heaven. Simon and his wife and children fell to the ground. Wings appeared upon the angel's shoulders, and he rose into the heavens.

And when Simon came to himself the hut stood as before, and there was no one in it but his own family.

"What Men Live By" was included in Leo Tolstoy's collection of short stories entitled *What Men Live By, and Other Tales*, published in 1885. It was first translated into English in 1906. It was then revised by the editors for inclusion in this edition.

Leo Tolstoy Bibliography (selected)

Novels and Novellas

Childhood (1852)
Boyhood (1854)
Youth (1856)
Family Happiness (1859)
The Cossacks (1863)
War and Peace (1869)
Anna Karenina (1878)
The Death of Ivan Ilyich (1886)
The Kreutzer Sonata (1889)
Resurrection (1899)
The Forged Coupon (1911)
Hadji Murat (1912)

Short stories

The Raid (1852)
The Snowstorm (1856)
Albert (1858)
Three Deaths (1859)
God Sees the Truth, But Waits (1872)

The Prisoner of the Caucasus (1872)
What Men Live By, and Other Tales (1885)
Quench the Spark (1885)
Where Love Is, God Is (1885)
Ivan the Fool (1885)
Wisdom of Children (1885)
The Three Hermits (1886)
Promoting a Devil (1886)
How Much Land Does a Man Need? (1886)
The Grain (1886)
Repentance (1886)
Croesus and Fate (1886)
Kholstomer (1886)
A Lost Opportunity (1889)
Master and Man (1895)
Too Dear! (1897)
Father Sergius (1898)
Work, Death, and Sickness (1903)
Three Questions (1903)
Alyosha the Pot (1905)
The Devil (1911)

Plays

The Power of Darkness (1886)
The Light Shines in the Darkness (1890)
The Fruits of Enlightenment (1891)
The Living Corpse (1900)

Non-Fiction

A Confession (1882)
The Gospel in Brief (1883)
What Is To Be Done? (1886)
The Kingdom of God Is Within You (1894)
What Is Art? (1897)

The Thoughts of Wise Men (1903; Russian: "Musli mudrykh liudei"), translated into English as Tolstoy's Words To Live By (2020) by Peter Sekirin

A Circle of Reading (1906; Russian: "Krug chteniia"), translated into English as A Calendar of Wisdom (1997) by Peter Sekirin

A Letter to a Hindu (1908)

Wise Thoughts for Every Day (1909; Russian: "Na kazhdyj den"), translated into English as Wise Thoughts for Every Day by Peter Sekirin

The Way of Life (1910)

Alan Twigg, left and Peter Sekirin, right

About the Translator and Editor

PETER SEKIRIN was born in Kiev. He has a Ph.D. in Comparative Literature from the University of Toronto. He has translated and edited works by and about Anton Chekhov and Fyodor Dostoevsky and also four books of Leo Tolstoy's non-fiction: *A Calendar of Wisdom*; *Wise Thoughts for Every Day; Divine and Human;* and now *Tolstoy's Words to Live By.* Peter lives in Aurora, Ontario.

ALAN TWIGG, founder of *BC BookWorld*, has written nineteen books and produced six films. His most recent book is a biography of a crusading female doctor, *Moon Madness: Dr. Louise Aall, Sixty Years of Healing in Africa*. He was inducted as a member of the Order of Canada in 2015. He lives in Vancouver, B.C. . Visit his website at www.alantwigg.com.